FOOD&WINE
Cocktails
2014

FOOD & WINE COCKTAILS 2014
EXECUTIVE EDITOR **Kate Krader**
DEPUTY EDITOR **Jim Meehan**
EDITOR **Susan Choung**
COPY EDITOR **Lisa Leventer**
RESEARCHER **Michelle Loayza**
EDITORIAL ASSISTANT **Sarah Kraut**

DESIGNER **Courtney Waddell Eckersley**
PRODUCTION MANAGERS
Matt Carson, Amelia Grohman
PRODUCTION ASSOCIATE **Pamela Brandt**

STYLIST **Alison Attenborough**
PHOTOGRAPHER **Frances Janisch**

AMERICAN EXPRESS PUBLISHING, A DIVISION OF TIME INC. AFFLUENT MEDIA GROUP
PRESIDENT/CHIEF EXECUTIVE OFFICER **Ed Kelly**
CHIEF MARKETING OFFICER/PRESIDENT,
DIGITAL MEDIA **Mark V. Stanich**
SVP/CHIEF FINANCIAL OFFICER **Paul B. Francis**
VPS/GENERAL MANAGERS
Frank Bland, Keith Strohmeier

VP, BOOKS & PRODUCTS/PUBLISHER **Marshall Corey**
DIRECTOR, BOOK PROGRAMS **Bruce Spanier**
SENIOR MARKETING MANAGER, BRANDED BOOKS
Eric Lucie
DIRECTOR OF FULFILLMENT & PREMIUM VALUE
Philip Black
MANAGER OF CUSTOMER SERVICE
& PRODUCT FULFILLMENT **Betsy Wilson**
DIRECTOR OF FINANCE **Thomas Noonan**
ASSOCIATE BUSINESS MANAGER **Uma Mahabir**
VP, OPERATIONS **Tracy Kelliher**
SENIOR MANAGER, CONTRACTS & RIGHTS **Jeniqua Moore**

SENIOR PRODUCTION MANAGER,
TIME HOME ENTERTAINMENT, INC. **Susan Chodakiewicz**

FOOD & WINE MAGAZINE
SVP/EDITOR IN CHIEF **Dana Cowin**
CREATIVE DIRECTOR **Stephen Scoble**
EXECUTIVE MANAGING EDITOR **Mary Ellen Ward**
EXECUTIVE EDITOR **Pamela Kaufman**
EXECUTIVE FOOD EDITOR **Tina Ujlaki**
EXECUTIVE WINE EDITOR **Ray Isle**
EXECUTIVE DIGITAL EDITOR **Rebecca Bauer**
DEPUTY EDITOR **Christine Quinlan**

FEATURES
RESTAURANT EDITOR **Kate Krader**
TRAVEL EDITOR **Gina Hamadey**
SENIOR WINE EDITOR **Megan Krigbaum**
MARKET EDITOR **Suzie Myers**
EDITORIAL ASSISTANTS
Maren Ellingboe, Chelsea Morse, M. Elizabeth Sheldon

FOOD
DEPUTY EDITOR **Kate Heddings**
TEST KITCHEN SENIOR EDITOR **Kay Chun**
ASSOCIATE EDITOR **Daniel Gritzer**
TEST KITCHEN ASSOCIATE EDITOR **Justin Chapple**
EDITORIAL ASSISTANT **Julia Heffelfinger**

ART
DESIGN DIRECTOR **Patricia Sanchez**
ASSOCIATE ART DIRECTOR **James Maikowski**
DESIGNER **Bianca Jackson**

PHOTO
DIRECTOR OF PHOTOGRAPHY **Fredrika Stjärne**
PHOTO EDITOR **Sara Parks**
ASSOCIATE PHOTO EDITOR **James Owens**
PHOTO ASSISTANT **Tomi Omololu-Lange**

COPY & RESEARCH
COPY CHIEF **Elizabeth Herr**
SENIOR COPY EDITOR **Ann Lien**
ASSOCIATE RESEARCH EDITOR **Erin Laverty**
ASSISTANT RESEARCH EDITOR **Joseph Harper**

PRODUCTION
PRODUCTION MANAGERS
Matt Carson, Amelia Grohman
PRODUCTION ASSISTANT **Chelsea Schiff**

DIGITAL MEDIA
FEATURES EDITOR **Alex Vallis**
SENIOR EDITOR **Lawrence Marcus**
ASSOCIATE ART DIRECTOR **Jooyoung Hsu**
ASSISTANT EDITOR **Justine Sterling**
EDITORIAL ASSISTANT **Brianna Wippman**

EDITORIAL CONTENT MANAGER
Kerianne Hansen

ASSISTANT TO THE EDITOR IN CHIEF
Jacqueline Westbrook

ON THE COVER **Maguey Sour, p. 85**

FOOD&WINE
Cocktails
2014

FOOD&WINE
BOOKS

American Express Publishing,
a division of Time Inc. Affluent Media Group, New York

CELERY KAMIKAZE,
P. 52

Contents

Foreword

In 2005, *Food & Wine* documented a major trend—the birth of a creative new cocktail culture along with the rise of the mixologist—and published our first-ever guide to the best drinks in the country. Every year since, we've picked the best and coolest cocktails for this book. For our anniversary

FLAVOR KEY

THESE SYMBOLS TELL WHAT TO EXPECT IN EACH DRINK.

STRONG	SWEET	TART	BITTER	FRUITY	FLORAL	SMOKY
HIGH ALCOHOL CONTENT BY VOLUME	SIMPLE SYRUP, HONEY, SWEET LIQUEURS OR MIXERS	LEMON, LIME OR OTHER CITRUS	BITTERS, CAMPARI OR OTHER BITTER LIQUEURS	BERRIES, MELONS, OTHER FRUIT OR FRUIT-BASED LIQUEURS	FLOWERS OR FLOWER-BASED LIQUEURS SUCH AS ST-GERMAIN	MEZCAL, PEATED SCOTCH OR OTHER SMOKY INGREDIENTS

edition, we took up the challenge of selecting our best drinks from the past 10 years–the recipes that anyone who cares about cocktails needs in his or her repertoire. The results show off an astonishing array of spirits, drink styles and talented innovators.
They also reflect a decade's worth of trends. In our first year, we noted a new interest in obscure classics and published the gin-based Pegu (p. 64); a few years later, smoky drinks like the mezcal-infused Bohemio (p. 82) grabbed everyone's attention. Here's to a magnificent decade of cocktails.

Dana Cowin
Editor in Chief
FOOD & WINE Magazine

Jim Meehan
Deputy Editor
FOOD & WINE Cocktails 2014

Glassware

1 Martini

A stemmed glass with a cone-shaped bowl for cocktails served straight up (drinks that are mixed with ice and then strained).

2 Rocks

A short, wide-mouthed glass for spirits served neat (without ice) and cocktails poured over ice. **Single rocks** glasses hold up to 6 ounces; **double rocks** glasses hold closer to 12 ounces.

3 Collins

A very tall, narrow glass often used for drinks that are served on ice and topped with soda.

4 Wineglass

A tall, slightly rounded, stemmed glass for wine-based cocktails. White wine glasses are a fine substitute for high-ball glasses and are also good for frozen drinks. Balloon-shaped red wine glasses are ideal for fruity cocktails as well as punches.

5 Highball

A tall, narrow glass that helps preserve the fizz in cocktails that are served with ice and topped with sparkling beverages such as club soda, tonic water or ginger beer.

6   7   8   9   10

6 Coupe

A shallow, wide-mouthed, stemmed glass primarily for small (short) and potent cocktails that are served straight up.

7 Pilsner

A tall, flared glass designed for beer. It's also good for serving oversize cocktails on ice or drinks with multiple garnishes.

8 Heatproof Glass

A durable ceramic or glass cup with a handle. Perfect for coffee spiked with whiskey or other spirits as well as toddies and other hot drinks.

9 Flute

A tall, slender, usually stemmed glass; its narrow shape helps keep cocktails topped with Champagne or sparkling wine effervescent.

10 Julep Cup

A short pewter or silver cup designed to keep juleps (minty, crushed-ice cocktails) cold.

Snifter (not pictured)

A wide-bowled glass for spirits served neat.

Home Bar Tools

1 Hawthorne Strainer   **2** Jigger   **3** Muddler   **4** Channel Knife   **5** Julep Strainer   **6** Citrus Juicer   **7** Waiter's Corkscrew

1 Hawthorne Strainer

The best all-purpose strainer. A semicircular spring ensures a spill-proof fit on a shaker. Look for a tightly coiled spring, which keeps muddled fruit and herbs out of drinks.

2 Jigger

A two-sided stainless steel measuring instrument for precise mixing. Look for one with ½- and 1-ounce cups. A shot glass with measures works well, too.

3 Muddler

A sturdy tool that's used to crush herbs, sugar cubes and fresh fruit; it's traditionally made of wood. Choose a muddler that can reach the bottom of a cocktail shaker; in a pinch, substitute a long-handled wooden spoon.

4 Channel Knife

A small, spoon-shaped knife with a metal tooth. Creates garnishes by turning citrus-fruit peels into long, thin twists.

5 Julep Strainer

The preferred device for straining cocktails from a mixing glass because it fits securely. Fine holes keep ice out of the drink.

6 Citrus Juicer

A metal or ceramic citrus press, available in a variety of sizes, that allows you to squeeze lemons, limes and oranges *à la minute*.

7 Waiter's Corkscrew

A pocketknife-like tool with an attached bottle opener. Bartenders prefer it to bulkier, more complicated corkscrews.

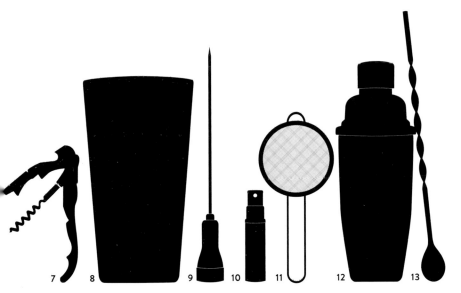

7   8   9   10   11   12   13

8 Boston Shaker

The bartender's choice; consists of a mixing glass, usually a pint glass, with a metal canister that covers the glass to create a seal. Shake drinks with the metal half pointing away from you.

9 Ice Pick

A sharp metal tool with a sturdy handle used to break off chunks from a larger block of ice.

10 Atomizer

A small spray bottle used to disperse tiny quantities of aromatic liquid evenly over the surface of an empty glass or on top of a cocktail. Atomizers are widely available at drugstores.

11 Fine Strainer

A fine-mesh strainer set over a glass before the cocktail is poured in (see Fine-Straining Drinks, p. 21). It keeps bits of muddled herbs, fruit and crushed ice out of drinks, resulting in a perfectly clear cocktail.

12 Cobbler Shaker

The most commonly used shaker, with a metal cup for mixing drinks with ice, a built-in strainer and a fitted top.

13 Bar Spoon

A long-handled metal spoon that mixes cocktails without creating air bubbles. Also useful for measuring small amounts of liquid.

Essential Spirits

Ten years ago, most bar drinks were vodka-based. Now almost any good cocktail list or well-stocked home bar includes these 11 choices.

Aperitifs (wine-based)

The word "aperitif" is often used to refer to any predinner drink, but aperitifs are also a category of beverage: light, dry and low-proof, with characteristic bitter flavors. A century ago, mixologists began adding wine-based aperitifs to cocktails instead of simply serving them on their own. Wine-based aperitifs include **dry vermouths,** above, and their relatives **quinquinas** (or kinas), such as Lillet and Dubonnet. These contain quinine, a bitter extract from cinnamon-like cinchona bark.

Aperitifs (spirit-based)

Low-proof, bitter, spirit-based aperitifs like Campari have always been popular in Europe. Now they're beloved in the US thanks to mixologists' embrace of bottles like Aperol, above, the bitter orange Italian *aperitivo.* Other examples of spirit-based aperitifs are Pimm's No. 1, a gin-based English aperitif with subtle spice and citrus flavors; and Cynar, which is made from 13 herbs and plants, including artichokes.

Absinthe

An herbal spirit, absinthe was banned in the US in 1912 in part because a key ingredient, wormwood, was thought to be toxic in large doses. In 2007 scientists concluded that modern bottlings are safe. High-quality absinthe is made much like gin: A neutral spirit is infused with botanicals such as fennel seed and anise. The distilled spirit can be either **clear** (blanche) or **green** (verte, above). Absinthe is often used in cocktails, as a rinse for a glass or splashed on top of a drink before serving.

Vodka

Produced all over the world, vodka is traditionally distilled from fermented grain or potatoes, but nearly any fruit or vegetable can be used, from grapes to beets. Most **flavored** vodkas are created by adding ingredients to a neutral spirit; the best macerate citrus, berries or herbs in high-proof alcohol. **Aquavit** is produced from a neutral alcohol and botanicals like caraway, citrus peel and star anise. Some are barrel-aged after distillation.

Gin

Gin is made by distilling a neutral grain spirit with botanicals such as juniper, coriander and citrus peels. The most ubiquitous style is **London dry,** above. It's bolder in flavor than the slightly sweet **Old Tom** gin, an 18th-century style of British gin. Two other types of the spirit are **Plymouth,** the British Royal Navy's preferred gin for nearly two centuries; and **New Western** gins, such as Hendrick's, which incorporate unusual botanicals like rose petals. **Genever** is a botanically rich, clear, malted grain–based spirit.

Tequila

The best tequila is made from 100 percent blue agave that is harvested by hand, slow-roasted in ovens, fermented with natural yeast, then distilled. **Blanco** (white) tequila is unaged. **Reposado** (rested) tequila, above, ages up to one year in barrels. **Añejo** (aged) tequila must be aged between one and three years. **Mezcal** is known for its smoky flavor, which comes from roasting the agave in earthen pits; the finest mezcals are unaged.

Rum

Distilled from cane syrup, molasses or fresh pressed sugarcane, rums are typically produced in tropical regions. **White,** a.k.a. silver or light, rums can be aged in wood for a short time. **Amber** (or gold) rum, above, is often aged in oak barrels for a short time; caramel is sometimes added for color. **Dark** rum is made with molasses; **spiced** rum is flavored with ingredients such as coconut, vanilla and cinnamon; and **rhum agricole** and **cachaça** are distilled from fresh sugarcane juice.

Whiskey

Whiskey is distilled from a fermented mash of grains such as malted barley, corn or rye and then matured in oak barrels (except for white whiskey). Scotland and Japan are famous for their **single malts** (produced from 100 percent malted barley from one distillery). Most smoky, peated whisky comes from **Islay** in Scotland. Canada favors **blended** whiskies high in rye. America is known for its **bourbon**, robust **rye** and unaged **white** whiskeys. **Irish** whiskeys, above, tend to be mellow blends.

Brandy

Brandies are distilled from a fermented mash of fruit. The best-known brandies are pot-distilled from wines that spend a long time in oak barrels before bottling. French brandies like **Armagnac** and **Cognac,** above, are named after the regions where they are made. **Applejack** is an American apple brandy blended with neutral spirits. Other styles include **pisco,** distilled from aromatic grapes in Peru and Chile; and **eau-de-vie,** a specialty of the European Alps, distilled from a fermented fruit mash and bottled without aging.

Amari

Amari ("bitters" in Italian) are bittersweet sipping spirits made by infusing or distilling a neutral spirit with herbs, spices, citrus peels or nuts before sweetening and bottling. Traditionally served after dinner to aid digestion, amari like Averna, Montenegro and Nonino, above, are popular with American bartenders for the complexity and balance they add to cocktails.

Liqueurs

Among the oldest spirits, liqueurs are produced from a base alcohol that's distilled or macerated with a variety of ingredients, then sweetened. Sugar makes up to 35 percent of a liqueur's weight by volume, and up to 40 percent for **crème liqueurs.** Liqueurs can be herbal (Chartreuse); citrus- or fruit-based (Cointreau); floral (violet-inflected parfait amour, above); or nut- or seed-based (Frangelico).

Bar Lexicon

AGAVE NECTAR A rich, sweet syrup made from the sap of the cactus-like agave plant.

ALLSPICE DRAM Also known as pimento dram; a rum-based liqueur infused with Jamaican allspice berries. **The Bitter Truth** and **St. Elizabeth** are good brands.

APEROL A vibrant orange-red, low-proof Italian *aperitivo* flavored with bitter orange, rhubarb, gentian and cinchona bark.

BAROLO CHINATO A Nebbiolo-based forti-fied wine (produced in Piedmont's Barolo zone) infused with cinchona bark (*china* in Italian) and various roots, herbs and spices, including rhubarb and cardamom.

BÉNÉDICTINE An herbal liqueur with flavors of hyssop, angelica, juniper and myrrh. According to legend, the recipe was developed by a French monk in 1510.

1 BITTERS A concentrated tincture of bitter and aromatic herbs, roots and spices that adds com-plexity to drinks. Varieties include orange, grape-fruit, cherry and aromatic bitters, the best known of which is **Angostura,** created in 1824. **Bitter-mens** makes bitters in unusual flavors like Xoco-latl Mole. **Fee Brothers** bitters come in 15 flavors and have been made in Rochester, New York, since the 1950s. **Peychaud's** bitters have flavors of anise and cherry; the recipe dates to 19th-century New Orleans.

BONAL GENTIANE-QUINA A slightly bitter French aperitif wine infused with gentian root and cin-chona bark, the source of quinine.

BRANCA MENTA A spin-off of the bitter Italian digestif Fernet-Branca (p. 18) with a pro-nounced peppermint and menthol flavor.

BYRRH GRAND QUINQUINA A mildly bitter French aperitif that combines red wine and lightly fermented grape juice with quinine-rich cinchona bark, bitter orange, coffee, cocoa and botanicals.

CAMPARI A potent, bright red Italian aperitif with a bitter orange flavor. It's made from fruit, herbs and spices.

1   **2**   **3**

2 CARPANO ANTICA FORMULA A rich and complex sweet red vermouth from Italy.

CHARTREUSE A spicy herbal French liqueur made from more than 100 botanicals; **green** Chartreuse is more potent than the honey-sweetened **yellow** one.

COCCHI AMERICANO A low-alcohol, white-wine-based Italian aperitif infused with cinchona bark, citrus peels and herbs such as gentian.

3 COCCHI VERMOUTH DI TORINO A slightly bitter, Moscato-based red vermouth from Italy with hints of citrus, rhubarb and cocoa.

COINTREAU A French triple sec that is made by macerating and distilling sun-dried sweet and bitter orange peels.

CRÈME DE CACAO A cacao-flavored liqueur that's often scented with vanilla. Less sweet than chocolate liqueur, it can be **dark** (brown) or **white** (colorless).

CRÉOLE SHRUBB A rhum agricole–based orange liqueur flavored with Creole spices and bitter orange peels.

CURAÇAO A general term for orange-flavored liqueurs historically produced in the French West Indies.

CYNAR A pleasantly bitter Italian *aperitivo* made from 13 herbs and plants, including artichokes.

DRAMBUIE A whisky-based Scottish liqueur flavored with honey, herbs and spices.

DUBONNET A wine-based, quinine-enhanced aperitif that comes in two varieties. The **rouge** is full-bodied. The drier **blanc** is a good substitute for dry vermouth.

FERNET-BRANCA A potent, bitter-flavored Italian digestif that's made from 27 herbs.

GALLIANO A golden Italian liqueur that includes some 30 herbs and spices, including lavender, anise, star anise, juniper and vanilla.

GUM SYRUP A simple syrup that's been thickened with gum arabic, a natural gum made from the sap of acacia trees.

HEERING CHERRY LIQUEUR A crimson-colored cherry liqueur made in Denmark since 1818. Heering is drier and more complex than other cherry liqueurs.

4 KINA L'AVION D'OR A deep golden Swiss aperitif made by infusing white wine with cinchona bark, orange peel, wormwood and spices.

5 KÜMMEL A grain-based liqueur first distilled in Holland in the late 1500s. It's flavored with caraway, cumin and fennel.

LICOR 43 A sweet Spanish liqueur with citrus and vanilla flavors.

LILLET A wine-based French aperitif flavored with orange peel and quinine. The **rouge** variety is sweeter than the **blanc.** The **rosé,** made from a blend of the red and white, has a slightly fruity flavor.

6 MARASCHINO LIQUEUR A colorless Italian liqueur. The best brands are distilled from sour marasca cherries and their pits, then aged in ash wood vats and sweetened with sugar.

ORGEAT A sweet, non-alcoholic syrup made from almonds or almond extract, sugar and rose or orange flower water.

PASTIS A licorice-flavored French spirit that turns cloudy when mixed with water. It's similar to absinthe (p. 13) but sweeter and lower in alcohol.

PIMM'S NO. 1 A gin-based English aperitif often served with ginger beer, 7-Up or lemonade.

POIRE WILLIAM A pear eau-de-vie, usually made in Switzerland or the Alsace region of France.

PORT A fortified wine from the Douro region of Portugal. Styles include fruity, young **ruby** port; richer, nuttier **tawny;** thick-textured, oak-aged **late bottled vintage (LBV);** and decadent **vintage** port, made from the best grapes in the best vintages. Dry **white** port is often served chilled, as an aperitif.

PUNT E MES A spicy, orange-accented sweet Italian vermouth fortified with bitters.

SHERRY A fortified wine from Spain's Jerez region. Varieties include dry styles like **fino** and **manzanilla;** nuttier, richer **amontillado** and **oloroso;** and viscous, sweet **Pedro Ximénez (PX)** and **cream** sherry. **East India** sherry falls between an oloroso and a PX in style.

4   5   6

SHOCHU A Japanese vodka-like spirit distilled from a variety of ingredients, such as rice, buckwheat or barley.

ST-GERMAIN A French liqueur created by blending macerated elderflower blossoms with eau-de-vie. It has hints of pear, peach and grapefruit zest.

STREGA An Italian liqueur infused with approximately 70 herbs and spices. One of them is saffron, which gives it a golden yellow color.

TRIPLE SEC An orange-flavored liqueur that is similar to curaçao but not as sweet. **Cointreau,** created in 1875, is the most famous. **Combier,** created in 1834, claims to be the world's first.

VERMOUTH An aromatic fortified wine. **Dry** vermouth is used in martinis. The **sweet** variety, which is usually red, is often used to make Manhattans. Sweet, white and aromatic Italian **bianco** and French **blanc** vermouths are traditionally served on the rocks. **Rosé** and **rosato** vermouths are pink, with a spicy flavor.

Keep vermouth in the refrigerator (up to three months) to retain its character.

VS Cognacs labeled **VS** (Very Special) are aged at least two years. **VSOP** (Very Superior Old Pale) Cognacs must be aged at least four years.

Mixology Basics

Making a Twist

A twist—a small piece of citrus zest—lends a drink concentrated citrus flavor from the peel's essential oils.

TO MAKE AND USE A STANDARD TWIST

1. Use a sharp paring knife or vegetable peeler to cut a thin, oval, quarter-size disk of the peel, avoiding the pith.

2. Grasp the outer edges skin side down and pinch the twist over the drink. Rub it around the glass rim, then drop it in.

TO MAKE A SPIRAL-CUT TWIST

1. Use a channel knife to cut a 3-inch-long piece of peel with some of the pith intact. Cut the twist over the glass so its essential oils fall into the drink.

2. Wrap the twist around a straw; tighten at both ends to create a curlicue shape.

Flaming a Twist

Flaming a lemon or orange twist caramelizes the zest's essential oils.

1. Make a standard twist. Gently grasp the outer edges, skin side down, between the thumb and two fingers and hold it about 4 inches over the cocktail.

2. Hold a lit match over the drink an inch away from the twist—don't let the flame touch the peel—then pinch the edges of the twist sharply so that the citrus oils fall through the flame and into the drink.

Rimming a Glass

1. Spread salt (preferably kosher), sugar or other powdered ingredient on a small plate.

2. Moisten the outer rim of the glass with a citrus-fruit wedge, water or a syrup; roll the outer rim on the plate until it is lightly coated, then tap to release any excess.

Perfecting Ice

The right ice is essential to preparing a balanced and attractive drink.

TO MAKE BIG BLOCKS OF ICE FOR PUNCH BOWLS, pour water into a large, shallow plastic container and freeze. To unmold, first warm the bottom of the container in hot water.

TO MAKE LARGE ICE CUBES FOR ROCKS GLASSES, use flexible silicone ice molds (available at *cocktailkingdom.com*). Or make a large block of ice in a loaf pan and use an ice pick to break off chunks the size you want.

TO MAKE CRUSHED ICE, cover cubes in a clean kitchen towel and pound with a wooden mallet or rolling pin.

TO MAKE CRACKED ICE, place an ice cube in the palm of your hand and tap it with the back of a bar spoon until it breaks into pieces.

TO MAKE CLEAR CUBES, fill ice trays with hot filtered water.

TO MAKE PERFECTLY SQUARE CUBES, use flexible silicone Perfect Cube ice trays, below (available at *surlatable.com*).

Smacking Herbs

To accentuate the aroma of fresh herbs used for garnish, clap them between your hands over the glass to release the essential oils into the drink.

Fine-Straining Drinks

To remove tiny fruit or herb particles:

1. Set a fine strainer over a serving glass.

2. Make the drink in a shaker or mixing glass, set a Hawthorne or julep strainer (p. 10) on top, then pour through both strainers into the serving glass.

Homemade Mixers

Simple Syrup

MAKES ABOUT 12 OUNCES
In a small saucepan, combine 8 ounces water and 1 cup sugar and bring to a boil. Simmer over moderate heat, stirring frequently, until the sugar dissolves, about 3 minutes. Remove from the heat and let cool. Transfer the syrup to a bottle or tightly covered glass jar and refrigerate for up to 1 month.

Rich Simple Syrup

MAKES ABOUT 8 OUNCES
In a small saucepan, combine 4 ounces water and 1 cup Demerara or other raw sugar and bring to a boil. Simmer over moderate heat, stirring, until the sugar dissolves, about 3 minutes. Remove from the heat and let cool. Transfer the syrup to a bottle or tightly covered glass jar and refrigerate for up to 1 month.

Vanilla Simple Syrup

MAKES ABOUT 12 OUNCES
In a small saucepan, combine 8 ounces water, 1 cup sugar and ½ split vanilla bean and bring to a boil. Simmer over moderate heat, stirring, until the sugar dissolves, about 3 minutes. Let cool, then strain the syrup into a bottle or tightly covered glass jar and refrigerate for up to 1 month.

Easiest Simple Syrup

MAKES ABOUT 12 OUNCES
In a bottle or jar with a tight-fitting lid, combine 8 ounces hot water with 1 cup superfine sugar and shake until the sugar dissolves. Let cool, then refrigerate for up to 1 month.

Homemade Grenadine

MAKES ABOUT 12 OUNCES
In a bottle or jar with a tight-fitting lid, shake 8 ounces unsweetened pomegranate juice with 1 cup sugar until the sugar dissolves. If desired, add ⅛ teaspoon orange flower water. Refrigerate for up to 2 weeks.

Honey Syrup

MAKES ABOUT 6 OUNCES
In a microwavable bottle or jar, heat 4 ounces honey in a microwave for about 30 seconds at high power. Add 2 ounces warm water, cover tightly and shake until the honey dissolves. (Alternatively, in a small saucepan, stir 4 ounces honey and 2 ounces water over moderate heat until the honey dissolves.) Let cool, then refrigerate for up to 1 month.

Conversion Chart

Measures for spirits and other liquids are given in fluid ounces.
Refer to the chart below for conversions.

CUP		OUNCE		TBSP		TSP
1 c	=	8 fl oz				
¾ c	=	6 fl oz				
⅔ c	=	5⅓ fl oz				
		5 fl oz	=	10 tbsp		
½ c	=	4 fl oz				
		3 fl oz	=	6 tbsp		
⅓ c	=	2⅔ fl oz				
¼ c	=	2 fl oz				
		1 fl oz	=	2 tbsp		
		½ fl oz	=	1 tbsp	=	3 tsp
		⅓ fl oz	=	⅔ tbsp	=	2 tsp
		¼ fl oz	=	½ tbsp	=	1½ tsp

1 OUNCE = ABOUT 32 DASHES   1 DASH = 4 TO 5 DROPS

Aperitifs

Trends of the decade ● Ten years ago, *F&W Cocktails* had no Aperitifs chapter; now the predinner drinks section is one of the most diverse. ● Popular cocktails such as the Americano and the Aperol Spritz help revive the dormant aperitif culture in America. ● Obscure bottled aperitifs like Cocchi Americano and Bonal develop cult followings. ● Bartenders begin treating high-quality vermouths with care to preserve freshness: buying half-bottles and chilling them between pours. ● Mixologists rediscover fortified wines (sherry, port, Madeira) to design low-proof cobblers, cups and punches.

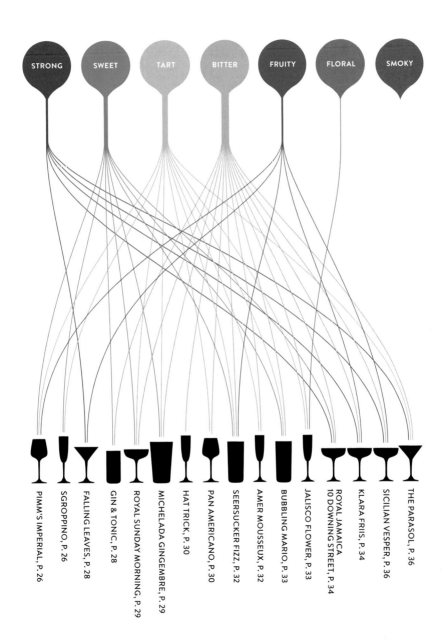

STRONG SWEET TART BITTER FRUITY FLORAL SMOKY

PIMM'S IMPERIAL, P. 26
SGROPPINO, P. 26
FALLING LEAVES, P. 28
GIN & TONIC, P. 28
ROYAL SUNDAY MORNING, P. 29
MICHELADA GINGEMBRE, P. 29
HAT TRICK, P. 30
PAN AMERICANO, P. 30
SEERSUCKER FIZZ, P. 32
AMER MOUSSEUX, P. 32
BUBBLING MARIO, P. 33
JALISCO FLOWER, P. 33
ROYAL JAMAICA 10 DOWNING STREET, P. 34
KLARA FRIIS, P. 34
SICILIAN VESPER, P. 36
THE PARASOL, P. 36

Pimm's Imperial

●●● | ⚷ | Makes: **1**

This upgraded Pimm's Cup from star mixologist Tony Abou-Ganim is topped with Champagne instead of the usual lemon soda or ginger ale. It's terrific as an alternative to mimosas at brunch.

1½ ounces Pimm's No. 1
    (gin-based English aperitif)
1 ounce fresh lemon juice
1 ounce Simple Syrup (p. 22)
    Ice
2 ounces chilled Champagne
1 cucumber spear, 1 thin apple slice, 1 small
    strawberry and 1 mint sprig, for garnish

In a cocktail shaker, combine the Pimm's, lemon juice and Simple Syrup; fill the shaker with ice and shake well. Strain into a chilled, ice-filled wineglass and stir in the Champagne. Garnish with the cucumber spear, apple slice, strawberry and mint sprig. —*Tony Abou-Ganim*

Sgroppino

●● | ⚷ | Makes: **1**

A traditional Venetian cocktail, the Sgroppino can be served as an aperitif or dessert. The sorbet is sometimes scooped on top, but George Schwarz of Manhattan's Temple Bar stirs it in, making the drink slushy and thoroughly chilled.

½ ounce citrus vodka
2 small scoops of lemon sorbet
¼ ounce fresh lemon juice
3 ounces chilled Prosecco

In a mixing glass, combine the vodka, sorbet and lemon juice and stir well. Add the Prosecco, stir again and pour into a chilled flute. —*George Schwarz*

PIMM'S IMPERIAL

Falling Leaves

●● | ∀ | Makes: **1**

Before Audrey Saunders opened Pegu Club in New York City, she ran the beverage program at The Carlyle hotel's famed Bemelmans Bar. Her signature drink there was this intensely aromatic wine-based cocktail.

2¼ ounces chilled dry Riesling
  1 ounce pear eau-de-vie
  ¼ ounce orange curaçao, preferably Marie Brizard
  ¼ ounce Honey Syrup (p. 22)
     Ice
  1 star anise pod, for garnish

In a cocktail shaker, combine the Riesling, eau-de-vie, curaçao and Honey Syrup; fill the shaker with ice and shake well. Strain into a chilled martini glass and garnish with the star anise. —*Audrey Saunders*

Gin & Tonic

●● | ▮ | Makes: **1**

Once a mainstay of country clubs, the gin and tonic has become a popular drink at US tapas restaurants. The trend started in Spain a few years ago.

1½ ounces gin, preferably Plymouth
  4 ounces chilled tonic water, preferably Fentimans
     Ice
1 or 2 lime wedges, for garnish

In a chilled highball glass, combine the gin and tonic water; fill the glass with ice and stir well. Garnish with the lime wedge. —*Todd Thrasher*

Royal Sunday Morning

2 ounces dry vermouth
¾ ounce fresh grapefruit juice
¾ teaspoon raspberry preserves
  Ice
1 ounce chilled dry sparkling wine
½ ounce chilled club soda

In a cocktail shaker, combine the vermouth, grape-fruit juice and preserves; fill the shaker with ice and shake well. Fine-strain (p. 21) into a chilled coupe and stir in the sparkling wine and club soda. —Sean Hoard

Note For a mocktail variation, see p. 164.

●●○ | 🍸 | Makes: **1**

Sean Hoard of The Commissary in Portland, Oregon, makes this cocktail for Sunday brunch at his parents' house. He shakes the drink with raspberry jam, which adds a velvety texture and gorgeous pink hue.

Michelada Gingembre

6 ounces chilled Sprite
1 ounce fresh lemon juice
1 ounce Simple Syrup (p. 22)
¾ ounce fresh ginger juice (from a 2-inch piece
   of ginger, grated and pressed through
   a fine strainer)
  Dash of jalapeño hot sauce
  Ice
12 ounces chilled IPA-style beer
  Pinch of sea salt

In a chilled pint glass, combine the Sprite, lemon juice, Simple Syrup, ginger juice and hot sauce; half-fill the glass with ice and stir well. Add enough beer to fill the glass and top with the salt. As you finish the drink, continue to pour in more beer. —Damian Windsor

●●○ | 🍺 | Makes: **1**

This drink is a mash-up of a shandy (a light lager mixed with lemonade or ginger beer) and a michelada (a Mexican beer cocktail). L.A.-based cocktail consultant Damian Windsor includes hoppy IPA, fresh ginger and a dash of hot sauce.

Hat Trick

● | ! | Makes: **1**

There are so many
more types of bitters
today beyond old
standbys like Angostura.
Jeff Grdinich of The
Rose in Jackson Hole,
Wyoming, uses rhubarb
bitters to enhance
Aperol, a versatile *aperitivo* flavored with bitter
orange and rhubarb.

1½ ounces amontillado sherry
1 ounce Aperol
2 dashes of Fee Brothers rhubarb bitters
or orange bitters, plus 1 dash for garnish
Ice
1½ ounces chilled Prosecco
1 lemon twist, for garnish

In a cocktail shaker, combine the sherry, Aperol and
2 dashes of bitters; fill the shaker with ice and shake
well. Strain into a chilled flute, stir in the Prosecco
and garnish with a dash of bitters and the lemon twist.
—*Jeff Grdinich*

Pan Americano

●● | ! | Makes: **1**

This spicy, botanical-
driven spritzer is from
mixologist Francesco
Lafranconi. Just like its
namesake highway,
the Pan Americano
embraces various cul-
tures and flavors:
Peruvian pisco, Italian
Aperol and the
French herbal liqueur
Chartreuse.

2 ounces chilled Sauvignon Blanc
or other crisp white wine
1 ounce chilled club soda
¾ ounce pisco
¾ ounce Aperol
¾ ounce yellow Chartreuse
Ice
One 2-inch strip of Ruby Red grapefruit zest,
for garnish

In a chilled wineglass, combine the wine, club soda,
pisco, Aperol and Chartreuse; fill the glass with
ice and stir well. Garnish with the grapefruit zest.
—*Francesco Lafranconi*

PAN AMERICANO

Seersucker Fizz

●●● | ▌ | Makes: **1**

Jim Romdall of Rumba in Seattle loves fortified wines in fizzes (sour-based cocktails with citrus juice and carbonated water). "A fizz is a wonderful way to bring the flavors out in bold vermouths and wine-based liqueurs," he says.

1 ounce **London dry gin**
1 ounce **Punt e Mes (spicy sweet vermouth)**
1 ounce **fresh lemon juice**
½ ounce **apricot liqueur**
¼ ounce **Simple Syrup (p. 22)**
1 large **egg white**
    Ice
2 ounces **chilled club soda**
1 **orange twist, preferably spiral-cut (p. 20), for garnish**

In a cocktail shaker, combine all of the ingredients except ice, the club soda and garnish; shake vigorously. Add ice and shake again. Fine-strain (p. 21) into a chilled collins glass, stir in the club soda and garnish with the twist. —*Jim Romdall*

Amer Mousseux

●● | ! | Makes: **1**

The two Italian liqueurs—Cynar and Campari—in this bubbly aperitif from Bouchon in Napa are famed for sparking the appetite.

1 ounce **Cynar**
½ ounce **Campari**
½ ounce **fresh orange juice**
    Ice
3 ounces **chilled Champagne**
1 **orange twist, for garnish**

In a cocktail shaker, combine the Cynar, Campari and orange juice; fill the shaker with ice and shake well. Strain into a chilled flute, stir in the Champagne and garnish with the orange twist. —*Bouchon, Yountville, California*

Bubbling Mario

1½ ounces vodka, preferably wheat,
    such as Russian Standard
1 ounce fresh lemon juice
1 ounce fresh orange juice
¾ ounce Aperol
½ ounce Honey Syrup (p. 22)
    Ice
1 ounce chilled Prosecco
1 orange wheel and 1 spiral-cut lemon twist
    (p. 20), for garnish

In a cocktail shaker, combine the vodka, citrus juices, Aperol and Honey Syrup; fill the shaker with ice and shake well. Strain into a chilled, ice-filled collins glass and stir in the Prosecco. Garnish with the orange wheel and lemon twist. —*Tony Abou-Ganim*

●●○ | ▌ | Makes: **1**

Mixology consultant Tony Abou-Ganim created this light, restorative drink for a golf event hosted by star chef Mario Batali. "A highlight was mixing one of these cocktails for President Clinton," Abou-Ganim says. "I do think he liked it!"

Jalisco Flower

1 ounce fresh Ruby Red grapefruit juice
¾ ounce St-Germain elderflower liqueur
½ ounce reposado tequila
    Ice
4 ounces chilled Prosecco

In a cocktail shaker, combine the grapefruit juice, St-Germain and tequila; fill the shaker with ice and shake well. Strain into a chilled flute and stir in the Prosecco. —*Vincenzo Marianella*

●●○ | ! | Makes: **1**

Vincenzo Marianella, head barman at Copa d'Oro in Santa Monica, California, custom-made this aperitif for a guest one evening. She ended up ordering three of them before dinner.

Royal Jamaica
10 Downing Street

●●● | ⊻ | Makes: **1**

French aperitif wines were developed to make antimalarial quinine go down easier for soldiers in the colonies. The Kina L'Avion d'Or that Boston mixologist Will Thompson uses here is based on a 19th-century recipe.

  2 ounces Kina L'Avion d'Or (slightly bitter
     aperitif wine)
  ½ ounce white overproof Jamaican rum
  ¼ ounce white crème de cacao
     Ice
  1 grapefruit twist, for garnish

In a mixing glass, combine the Kina, rum and crème de cacao; fill the glass with ice and stir well. Strain into a chilled coupe and garnish with the grapefruit twist.
—*Will Thompson*

Klara Friis

●●● | ⊻ | Makes: **1**

"I loved the Clara Frijs pears that my mom used to serve us in the autumn," says Copenhagen mixologist Søren Krogh Sørensen. "The Poire William in this drink triggers the same joy."

 2½ ounces oloroso sherry
  ¾ ounce Poire William (pear eau-de-vie)
  ¾ ounce aquavit (caraway-flavored distilled spirit)
     Dash of grapefruit bitters
     Ice

In a mixing glass, combine the sherry, Poire William, aquavit and bitters; fill the glass with ice and stir well. Strain into a chilled coupe. —*Søren Krogh Sørensen*

ROYAL JAMAICA
10 DOWNING STREET

Sicilian Vesper

●●○ | ▼ | Makes: **1**

Vesper refers to the period when afternoon segues into evening— aperitif time. Jamie Boudreau of Seattle's Canon makes this drink with Sicilian Marsala, giving it a dry, nutty quality.

2 ounces dry Marsala
½ ounce Poire William (pear eau-de-vie)
¼ ounce cream sherry
    Dash of Angostura bitters
    Ice

In a mixing glass, combine the Marsala, Poire William, sherry and bitters; fill the glass with ice and stir well. Strain into a chilled coupe. —*Jamie Boudreau*

The Parasol

●○○ | ▼ | Makes: **1**

When The Parasol was first served at The John Dory in Manhattan, Francis Schott—the drink's creator and one half of *The Restaurant Guys* radio show—had dinner there. "Just for fun, I asked the bartender about the drink. He said it was the chef's favorite cocktail." Schott smiled and ordered one with a *bottarga* starter. "It was a delicious combination."

2 ounces Aperol
1 ounce pisco
¾ ounce Simple Syrup (p. 22)
½ ounce fresh lemon juice
½ ounce fresh lime juice
1 large egg white
    Ice
4 drops of Angostura bitters, for garnish

In a cocktail shaker, combine the Aperol, pisco, Simple Syrup, citrus juices and egg white and shake vigorously. Fill the shaker with ice and shake again. Strain into a chilled martini glass. Drop the bitters onto the surface of the drink in the pattern of a square and swirl gently with a straw or toothpick to make a design in the foamy head. —*Francis Schott*

SICILIAN VESPER

Vodka

Trends of the decade ● Modern distillers redefine the spirit (which by legal definition is flavorless) by creating versions full of character. ● Craft producers take over the top shelf at bars–once the sole domain of the big brands. ● In addition to vodkas with flavors like blood orange, double espresso and black truffle, vodka makers unleash spirits weirdly infused with ingredients like tobacco. ●Vodka houses launch vintage vodkas, estate-grown grains and distillery tours.

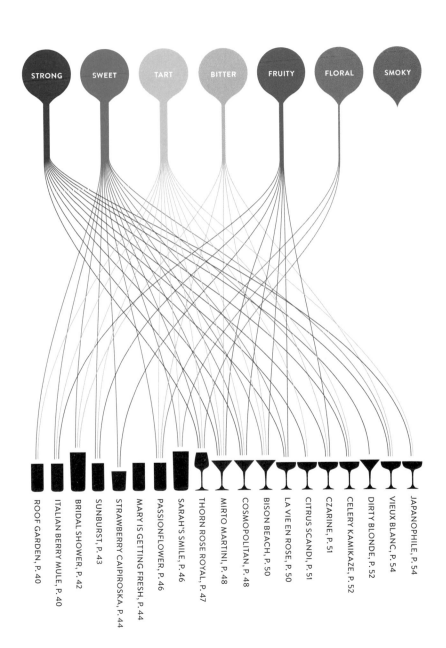

STRONG SWEET TART BITTER FRUITY FLORAL SMOKY

ROOF GARDEN, P. 40
ITALIAN BERRY MULE, P. 40
BRIDAL SHOWER, P. 42
SUNBURST, P. 43
STRAWBERRY CAIPIROSKA, P. 44
MARY IS GETTING FRESH, P. 44
PASSIONFLOWER, P. 46
SARAH'S SMILE, P. 46
THORN ROSE ROYAL, P. 47
MIRTO MARTINI, P. 48
COSMOPOLITAN, P. 48
BISON BEACH, P. 50
LA VIE EN ROSE, P. 50
CITRUS SCANDI, P. 51
CZARINE, P. 51
CELERY KAMIKAZE, P. 52
DIRTY BLONDE, P. 52
VIEUX BLANC, P. 54
JAPANOPHILE, P. 54

Roof Garden

●● | ▮ | Makes: **1**

An abundance of mint and thyme—two herbs that thrive in urban rooftop gardens—makes this drink ultra-refreshing.

15 mint leaves, plus 1 mint sprig for garnish
 2 thyme sprigs
¾ ounce Simple Syrup (p. 22)
 2 ounces vodka
 1 ounce fresh lemon juice
    Ice
 1 ounce chilled club soda

In a cocktail shaker, muddle the mint leaves with the thyme sprigs and Simple Syrup. Add the vodka and lemon juice; fill the shaker with ice and shake well. Fine-strain (p. 21) into a chilled, ice-filled highball glass, stir in the club soda and garnish with the mint sprig. —*Grace, Los Angeles (now closed)*

Italian Berry Mule

●●● | ▮ | Makes: **1**

"Berries and balsamic work so well together in food that it would be crazy not to try the combination in a drink," says mixology consultant Philip Duff. The quality of the ginger beer is important; Duff prefers Goya brand for its spiciness.

 6 raspberries
 2 ounces vodka
½ ounce fresh lime juice
¼ ounce Rich Simple Syrup (p. 22)
½ teaspoon aged balsamic vinegar
    Ice
 2 ounces chilled ginger beer

In a cocktail shaker, muddle the raspberries. Add the vodka, lime juice, Rich Simple Syrup and vinegar; fill the shaker with ice and shake well. Strain the drink into a chilled, ice-filled highball glass and stir in the ginger beer. —*Philip Duff*

ROOF GARDEN
"Camilla" highball tumbler
by William Yeoward.

Bridal Shower

●●● | ❙ | Makes: **1**

Time: **15 min** plus
baking and cooling

Mike Ryan, head
bartender at Chicago's
Sable Kitchen & Bar,
likes to use a neutral
spirit like vodka to
showcase the subtle,
earthy bitterness of the
rhubarb in the syrup.
Any leftover syrup
is fabulous mixed with
seltzer for a pretty
homemade soda.

2 **ounces vodka**
¾ **ounce Rhubarb Syrup (below)**
¾ **ounce fresh lemon juice**
¼ **ounce Campari**
   **Dash of Fee Brothers Old Fashion aromatic bitters
   or Angostura bitters**
   Ice
1 **ounce chilled club soda**
2 **long, thin slices of rhubarb stalk, for garnish**

In a cocktail shaker, combine the vodka, Rhubarb
Syrup, lemon juice, Campari and bitters; fill the
shaker with ice and shake well. Strain into a chilled,
ice-filled collins glass and stir in the club soda.
Garnish with the rhubarb.

RHUBARB SYRUP

In a glass baking dish, combine ½ pound chopped
rhubarb with 1 cup sugar, 8 ounces water and a pinch
of salt. Bake in a preheated 325° oven for 1 hour,
stirring every 15 minutes, until the rhubarb is very
tender. Let cool, then press through a fine strainer
into a jar. Cover and refrigerate the syrup for up to
1 week. Makes about 12 ounces. —*Mike Ryan*

Sunburst

½ kiwi, peeled and quartered,
   plus 1 or 2 kiwi slices for garnish
2 ounces vodka
1 ounce Tangerine Syrup (below)
½ ounce Aperol
   Ice
1 ounce chilled club soda
1 tangerine wheel, for garnish

In a cocktail shaker, muddle the quartered kiwi. Add the vodka, Tangerine Syrup and Aperol; fill the shaker with ice and shake well. Strain into a chilled, ice-filled highball glass, stir in the club soda and garnish with the kiwi slices and tangerine wheel.

TANGERINE SYRUP

In a small saucepan, combine 8 ounces fresh tangerine juice with 1 cup sugar. Bring to a boil over moderately high heat, stirring to dissolve the sugar, about 3 minutes. Let cool completely, then transfer to a jar, cover and refrigerate the syrup for up to 1 week. Makes about 12 ounces. —H. Joseph Ehrmann

●●● | ▮ | Makes: **1**

When H. Joseph Ehrmann of Elixir in San Francisco created this cocktail in 2009, he employed a number of techniques that most bartenders considered too cumbersome at the time: muddling fresh seasonal produce and making his own tangerine syrup.

Strawberry Caipiroska

●● | ▪ | Makes: **1**

The vodka-based caipiroska is a Russified twist on Brazil's classic caipirinha, made with cachaça (a spirit distilled from sugarcane).

½ lime, cut into quarters
1 heaping cup strawberries, hulled
1 tablespoon sugar
2 ounces vodka
  Ice
2 ounces chilled Sprite or club soda (optional)

In a cocktail shaker, muddle the lime with all but 1 of the strawberries and the sugar until the berries are juicy. Add the vodka and enough ice to fill a rocks glass. Shake briefly to chill, then pour—don't strain—into a chilled rocks glass. Stir in the soda and garnish with the reserved strawberry. —*Patricio Maciel*

Mary Is Getting Fresh

▪ | Makes: **1**

This light and fresh variation on the Bloody Mary has a rather zany origin: A freewheeling party guest added vodka to a near-empty bowl of salsa. In the more refined incarnation here, Todd Thrasher of Restaurant Eve in Alexandria, Virginia, mixes vodka with fresh tomato, onion, jalapeño and cilantro.

1 small plum tomato
1 lemon wedge
1 lime wedge
1 teaspoon diced red onion
1 teaspoon diced seeded jalapeño
1 teaspoon prepared horseradish
4 cilantro sprigs
  Dash of Worcestershire sauce
  Pinch each of salt and freshly ground pepper
2 ounces vodka
  Ice

In a cocktail shaker, muddle all of the ingredients except the vodka and ice. Add the vodka, fill the shaker with ice and shake well. Strain into a chilled, ice-filled highball glass. —*Todd Thrasher*

STRAWBERRY CAIPIROSKA

"Eleanor" tumbler by William Yeoward.

Passionflower

●●●● | ❚ | Makes: **1**

This cocktail from Las Vegas mixologist Ray Srp gets its "passion" from parfait amour ("perfect love"), a purple French liqueur flavored with orange peel, violets and vanilla.

1½ ounces citrus vodka
¾ ounce Campari
¾ ounce fresh lemon juice
½ ounce parfait amour (purple-hued, violet-flavored liqueur)
1 large egg white
Ice
1 edible orchid or 1 lime wheel, for garnish

In a cocktail shaker, combine the vodka, Campari, lemon juice, parfait amour and egg white; shake vigorously. Fill the shaker with ice and shake again. Strain into a chilled, ice-filled highball glass and garnish with the orchid. —*Ray Srp*

Sarah's Smile

●●● | ❚ | Makes: **1**

Tony Abou-Ganim, author of *Vodka Distilled*, created Sarah's Smile for his best friend's wife on her 50th birthday. The drink is great for parties because it can be prepared in advance in large batches and the flavors are almost universally loved.

1½ ounces vodka, preferably grape, such as Cîroc
1 ounce St-Germain elderflower liqueur
1 ounce fresh Ruby Red grapefruit juice
1 ounce fresh lemon juice
½ ounce Aperol
½ ounce Simple Syrup (p. 22)
Ice
1 Ruby Red grapefruit wheel and 1 mint sprig, for garnish

In a cocktail shaker, combine the vodka, St-Germain, citrus juices, Aperol and Simple Syrup; fill the shaker with ice and shake well. Strain into a chilled, ice-filled collins glass and garnish with the grapefruit wheel and mint sprig. —*Tony Abou-Ganim*

Thorn Rose Royal

1   thin quarter-size slice of fresh ginger
¾   ounce Simple Syrup (p. 22)
2   ounces Jasmine Tea–Infused Vodka (below)
¾   ounce fresh lemon juice
½   teaspoon maraschino liqueur
       Ice
1½   ounces chilled rosé Champagne or
       sparkling wine
1   lemon wheel, for garnish

In a cocktail shaker, muddle the ginger with the Simple Syrup. Add the infused vodka, lemon juice and maraschino liqueur; fill the shaker with ice and shake well. Strain into a chilled, ice-filled wineglass, stir in the Champagne and garnish with the lemon wheel.

JASMINE TEA–INFUSED VODKA

In a jar, cover 1 jasmine tea bag with 3 ounces vodka. Let the vodka steep for 10 minutes. Discard the tea bag. Cover and store the infused vodka at room temperature for up to 1 month. Makes 3 ounces. —*Ivy Mix*

 | ♟ | Makes: **1**

A cold remedy of jasmine green tea, ginger and lemon spawned the idea for this lovely cocktail. Ivy Mix, bartender at Clover Club in Brooklyn, New York, makes a quick infused vodka with jasmine tea pearls, but a simple tea bag works well, too.

Mirto Martini

●●○●●　|　Ᵽ　|　Makes: **1**

Served as a welcome cocktail at Arcodoro in Houston, this drink features mirto, a bitter myrtle berry digestif. Owner Efisio Farris makes his own mirto; bottled mirto is increasingly available in spirits shops.

1　ounce orange vodka
¾　ounce mirto
¾　ounce fresh lime juice
½　ounce Cointreau or other triple sec
¼　ounce Simple Syrup (p. 22)
　　Ice
4　blueberries skewered on a pick, for garnish

In a cocktail shaker, combine the vodka, mirto, lime juice, Cointreau and Simple Syrup; fill the shaker with ice and shake well. Strain into a chilled martini glass and garnish with the skewered blueberries. —*Efisio Farris*

Cosmopolitan

●●●○●　|　Ᵽ　|　Makes: **1**

Many credit this iconic 1990s cocktail to Toby Cecchini, a former bartender at The Odeon in Manhattan. Cecchini, author of the memoir *Cosmopolitan: A Bartender's Life*, recalls creating the drink in 1988. Bartenders today still rely on his recipe, using just enough cranberry juice to provide the sheerest pink color.

2½ ounces lemon vodka
1　ounce triple sec
1　ounce chilled cranberry juice
1½ teaspoons fresh lime juice
　　Ice
1　lemon twist, preferably spiral-cut (p. 20), for garnish

In a cocktail shaker, combine the vodka, triple sec and cranberry and lime juices; fill the shaker with ice and shake well. Strain into a chilled martini glass and garnish with the lemon twist. —*Classic*

COSMOPOLITAN
"Vinum XL" martini
glass by Riedel.

Bison Beach

●●●● | ❧ | Makes: **1**

Miami bartender John Lermayer uses Żubrówka, a bison grass–flavored vodka, in his cocktail. Bison grass, native to Poland and Belarus, has distinctive vanilla and herbal aromas.

 2 ounces chilled unsweetened apple cider
1½ ounces vodka, preferably bison grass
 ¾ ounce Aperol
 ¾ ounce fresh lemon juice
    Ice
 1 orange twist, for garnish

In a cocktail shaker, combine the cider, vodka, Aperol and lemon juice; fill the shaker with ice and shake well. Strain into a chilled martini glass and garnish with the orange twist. —*John Lermayer*

La Vie en Rose

●●● | ❧ | Makes: **1**

To add fruity flavor without sweetness to cocktails, Chicago mixology consultant Tim Lacey uses good-quality framboise (raspberry eau-de-vie). According to legend, eau-de-vie ("water of life") was invented by a 17th-century monk when he cooked fermented cherries as a cure for cholera.

1½ teaspoons rosemary leaves
 ½ ounce Simple Syrup (p. 22)
1½ ounces vodka
 1 ounce framboise
 1 ounce Lillet blanc
    Ice
 1 raspberry, for garnish

In a mixing glass, muddle the rosemary with the Simple Syrup. Add the vodka, framboise and Lillet; fill the glass with ice and stir well. Fine-strain (p. 21) into a chilled coupe and garnish with the raspberry. —*Tim Lacey*

Citrus Scandi

1 orange wedge
1½ ounces vodka
¾ ounce fresh grapefruit juice
¼ ounce aquavit (caraway-flavored distilled spirit)
¼ ounce Cointreau or other triple sec
¼ ounce Simple Syrup (p. 22)
   Ice
1 orange twist

Squeeze the orange wedge into a cocktail shaker, drop it in, then add the vodka, grapefruit juice, aquavit, Cointreau and Simple Syrup. Fill the shaker with ice and shake well. Strain into a chilled coupe or 2 shot glasses; pinch the orange twist over the drink and discard. —*Kathy Casey*

 | ☈ | Makes: **1**

Kathy Casey of the web cocktail show *Kathy Casey's Liquid Kitchen* likes to pair this drink with fresh shucked oysters. She puts a little aquavit in a small mister and spritzes the oysters just before serving them.

Czarine

1½ ounces frozen vodka
½ ounce dry vermouth
2½ teaspoons apricot liqueur
   Dash of Angostura bitters
   Cracked ice (p. 21)

In a mixing glass, combine the vodka, vermouth, apricot liqueur and bitters; fill the glass with cracked ice and stir well. Strain the drink into a chilled coupe. —*Hidetsugu Ueno*

●● | ☈ | Makes: **1**

To keep this classic drink from getting too cold, Hidetsugu Ueno of Bar High Five in Tokyo employs what he calls a low-speed stir. "You have to know when the stir feels heavy in your hand," he says. "That's the moment when the apricot aroma really comes through in the drink."

Celery Kamikaze

●●○ | ⊼ | Makes: **1**

Kevin Ludwig, bartender at La Taq in Portland, Oregon, adds pepper vodka and celery juice to the typically sweet-tart kamikaze, giving it a spicy-savory kick.

1   **lime wedge and kosher salt**
2   **ounces pepper vodka**
1   **ounce fresh lime juice**
1   **ounce celery juice**
½ **ounce Cointreau or other triple sec**
½ **ounce Simple Syrup (p. 22)**
   Ice

Moisten half of the outer rim of a chilled coupe with the lime wedge and coat lightly with salt. In a cocktail shaker, combine the vodka, lime and celery juices, Cointreau and Simple Syrup; fill the shaker with ice and shake well. Strain into the prepared coupe.
—*Kevin Ludwig*

Dirty Blonde

● | ⊼ | Makes: **1**

This riff on a dirty martini is made "blonde" with the addition of Lillet blanc, an amber French aperitif wine with hints of orange.

2   **ounces vodka**
¾ **ounce Lillet blanc**
3   **green olives for garnish, plus ¼ ounce brine from the jar**
   Ice

In a mixing glass, combine the vodka, Lillet and olive brine; fill with ice and stir well. Strain into a chilled martini glass and garnish with the olives.
—*Butter, Chicago (now closed)*

CELERY KAMIKAZE

Vieux Blanc

●●● | ʇ | Makes: **1**

San Francisco mixologist Joel Teitelbaum loves re-creating dark-spirit-based cocktails, such as the rye-based Vieux Carré, with clear spirits like vodka. "With all the new bitters available, you can do this with almost any classically dark cocktail," he says.

1½ ounces vodka, preferably rye, such as Bols
¾ ounce pisco
¾ ounce French blanc vermouth, such as Dolin
¼ ounce Galliano (Italian herbal liqueur)
¼ ounce Bénédictine (spiced herbal liqueur)
2 dashes of lemon bitters
  Ice
1 lemon twist, for garnish

In a mixing glass, combine all of the ingredients except ice and the twist; fill the glass with ice and stir well. Strain into a chilled coupe, then pinch the twist over the drink and drop it in. —*Joel Teitelbaum*

Japanophile

●● | ʇ | Makes: **1**

This drink is from John deBary, the bar director for the Momofuku restaurant group and assistant editor/tester for *F&W Cocktails 2013*. Reflecting deBary's near-lifelong fascination with Japanese culture, the cocktail uses mostly Japanese ingredients: sake, *shochu* (a clear distilled spirit similar to vodka) and tart yuzu juice.

¾ ounce aquavit
¾ ounce barley *shochu*
¾ ounce *daiginjo* or *ginjo* sake
½ ounce fresh orange juice
½ ounce yuzu juice (see Note)
½ teaspoon cane syrup (see Note) or Simple Syrup (p. 22)
  Ice

In a cocktail shaker, combine the aquavit, *shochu,* sake, orange and yuzu juices and cane syrup; fill the shaker with ice and shake well. Strain into a chilled coupe. —*John deBary*

Note If fresh yuzu isn't available, look for bottled yuzu juice at Japanese markets. Sweet, thick cane syrup is available at Whole Foods and *cocktailkingdom.com.*

VIEUX BLANC

"Fern" Champagne coupe
by William Yeoward.

Gin

Trends of the decade ● The number of small-batch gins in the US explodes, including Genevieve from Anchor and Aviation from House Spirits Distillery. ● New styles of gin that are less aggressively piney convert vodka drinkers. ● Old-fashioned styles reemerge: Old Tom (lightly sweetened), Navy-strength (extra-potent) and genever (malty; gin's Dutch progenitor). ● Mixologists begin barrel-aging gin cocktails like the Negroni. ● Distillers such as Citadelle and Beefeater start selling aged gins.

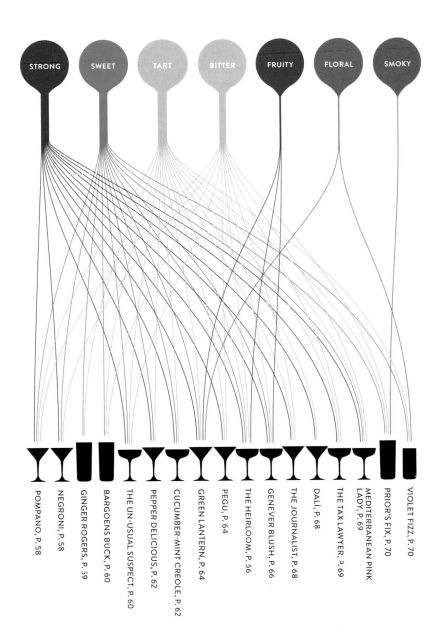

STRONG SWEET TART BITTER FRUITY FLORAL SMOKY

POMPANO, P. 58

NEGRONI, P. 58

GINGER ROGERS, P. 59

BARGOENS BUCK, P. 60

THE UN-USUAL SUSPECT, P. 60

PEPPER DELICIOUS, P. 62

CUCUMBER-MINT CREOLE, P. 62

GREEN LANTERN, P. 64

PEGU, P. 64

THE HEIRLOOM, P. 56

GENEVER BLUSH, P. 66

THE JOURNALIST, P. 68

DALÌ, P. 68

THE TAX LAWYER, P. 69

MEDITERRANEAN PINK LADY, P. 69

PRIOR'S FIX, P. 70

VIOLET FIZZ, P. 70

Pompano

●●●●● | ⟨ | Makes: **1**

Mixology consultant Nick Mautone describes the Pompano as a classic cocktail with the flavors of South Florida: It's fresh, with hints of fruit.

2   ounces gin, preferably Tanqueray No. Ten
1½ ounces fresh grapefruit juice
½   ounce sweet vermouth
      Dash of orange bitters
      Ice

In a cocktail shaker, combine the gin, grapefruit juice, vermouth and bitters; fill the shaker with ice and shake well. Strain into a chilled martini glass.
—Nick Mautone

Negroni

●●●● | ⟨ | Makes: **1**

Dating back to 1919, the Negroni is being rediscovered by a new generation of drinkers. Its recent popularity and appeal at all hours of the day—not just before dinner—has spawned the hashtag #negronioclock on Twitter and Instagram.

1   ounce gin, preferably London dry
1   ounce Campari
1   ounce sweet vermouth
      Ice
1   orange twist, for garnish

In a mixing glass, combine the gin, Campari and vermouth; fill the glass with ice and stir well. Strain into a chilled martini glass or coupe and garnish with the orange twist. Alternatively, strain into a chilled, ice-filled rocks glass and garnish. —Classic

Ginger Rogers

6 to 8 mint leaves, plus 1 mint
sprig for garnish
⅔   ounce Ginger-Pepper Syrup (below)
1½ ounces gin, preferably Plymouth
¾   ounce fresh lemon juice
Crushed ice (p. 21)
2   ounces chilled ginger ale

In a chilled collins glass, muddle the mint leaves
with the Ginger-Pepper Syrup. Add the gin and
lemon juice, then fill the glass with crushed ice. Spin
a swizzle stick or bar spoon between your hands
to mix the drink. Stir in the ginger ale, top with more
crushed ice and garnish with the mint sprig.

GINGER-PEPPER SYRUP

Thinly slice a 1-inch piece of ginger. In a small saucepan, combine ½ cup sugar with 6 ounces water,
1 teaspoon whole black peppercorns and the ginger.
Simmer over moderate heat, stirring, until the sugar
dissolves. Cook over low heat for 10 minutes. Remove
from the heat and let cool. Strain the syrup into a jar,
cover and refrigerate for up to 2 weeks. Makes about
8 ounces. —*Kathy Flick and Marcovaldo Dionysos*

 | | Makes: **1**

The Ginger Rogers
has been a best seller
at San Francisco's
Absinthe Bar & Brasse-
rie since the day the
place opened in 1998.
The key is an intense
ginger-pepper syrup
that amps up the gin-
ger ale flavor. "It's
like a mojito dancing
backwards in high
heels," says Marcovaldo
Dionysos, a former
bartender at Absinthe.

Bargoens Buck

●●● | ▮ | Makes: **1**

Bargoens Buck was the first drink L.A. mixologist Lindsay Nader made with Bols genever, produced in Amsterdam since 1664. The name is a nod to that era: "Bargoens" refers to a Dutch slang spoken in the 17th century, mainly by thieves and drifters.

1½ ounces genever, preferably Bols
¾ ounce fresh lemon juice
½ ounce Gran Classico Bitter
    (bittersweet herbal liqueur)
 2 dashes of Angostura bitters
    Ice
 1 ounce chilled ginger ale
½ orange wheel, for garnish

In a cocktail shaker, combine the genever, lemon juice, Gran Classico and bitters; fill the shaker with ice and shake well. Strain into a chilled, ice-filled collins glass, stir in the ginger ale and garnish with the orange wheel half. —*Lindsay Nader*

The Un-Usual Suspect

●●●● | ᵀ | Makes: **1**

Seattle bartender Kai Braaten creates this Negroni alternative with Fernet-Branca, a bracing herbal Italian bitter that has become a favorite ingredient of mixologists.

1½ ounces gin, preferably London dry
¾ ounce fresh grapefruit juice
½ ounce Drambuie
¼ ounce Honey Syrup (p. 22)
¼ ounce fresh lemon juice
¾ teaspoon Fernet-Branca
    Dash of Angostura bitters
    Ice
 1 grapefruit twist, for garnish

In a cocktail shaker, combine all of the ingredients except ice and the twist; fill the shaker with ice and shake well. Strain the drink into a chilled coupe and garnish with the grapefruit twist. —*Kai Braaten*

BARGOENS BUCK

Pepper Delicious

●●○ | ⏐ Y ⏐ Makes: **1**

Ryan Magarian came up with this riff on a gin gimlet when he was the bartender at Canlis restaurant in Seattle. Magarian went on to cofound Aviation gin, a New Western gin that includes lavender and cardamom in addition to the classic juniper.

12 to 15 mint leaves, plus 1 large mint sprig
    for garnish (optional)
¾ ounce Simple Syrup (p. 22)
 2 ounces gin, preferably Aviation
 1 ounce fresh lime juice
½ ounce fresh red bell pepper juice
    Ice
 1 red bell pepper ring, for garnish

In a cocktail shaker, muddle the mint leaves with the Simple Syrup. Add the gin, lime juice and pepper juice; fill the shaker with ice and shake well. Fine-strain (p. 21) into a chilled martini glass and garnish with the pepper ring and mint sprig.
—*Ryan Magarian*

Cucumber-Mint Creole

●●○ | ⏐ Y ⏐ Makes: **1**

Cucumber and mint are natural matches for herbaceous spirits like gin. Audrey Saunders, founder of Manhattan's Pegu Club, makes this drink with Plymouth gin.

 2 mint sprigs
 4 unpeeled cucumber wheels
¾ ounce fresh lemon juice
½ ounce Simple Syrup (p. 22)
1½ ounces gin, preferably Plymouth
½ ounce Dry Sack medium sherry
½ ounce cask-aged aquavit (caraway-flavored
    distilled spirit), preferably Linie
    Ice

In a mixing glass, muddle the leaves from 1 of the mint sprigs with 3 of the cucumber wheels, the lemon juice and the Simple Syrup. Add the gin, sherry and aquavit; fill the glass with ice and stir well. Fine-strain (p. 21) the drink into a chilled coupe and garnish with the remaining mint sprig and cucumber wheel.
—*Audrey Saunders*

PEPPER DELICIOUS
"Vinum XL" martini
glass by Riedel.

Green Lantern

●●●●● | ⟨ | Makes: **1**

Kiwi, a fruit often over-looked in cocktails, adds a lovely green hue to this drink that Thomas Waugh created at Range in San Francisco. He now oversees the cocktail program at ZZ's Clam Bar in Manhattan.

½ **kiwi, peeled and diced, plus 1 or 2 kiwi slices skewered on a pick for garnish**
¼ **ounce Simple Syrup (p. 22)**
1½ **ounces gin, preferably Hendrick's**
1 **ounce chilled Viognier**
½ **ounce fresh lime juice**
   Ice

In a cocktail shaker, muddle the diced kiwi with the Simple Syrup. Add the gin, Viognier and lime juice; fill the shaker with ice and shake well. Strain into a chilled martini glass and garnish with the skewered kiwi slices. —*Thomas Waugh*

Pegu

●●● | ⟨ | Makes: **1**

At Pegu Club in New York City, co-owner Audrey Saunders likes to mix this classic with a more assertive gin, like the high-proof Tanqueray.

2 **ounces gin, preferably London dry**
¾ **ounce orange curaçao**
¾ **ounce fresh lime juice**
   Dash of Angostura bitters
   Dash of orange bitters
   Ice
1 **lime wedge skewered on a pick, for garnish**

In a cocktail shaker, combine the gin, curaçao, lime juice and both bitters; fill the shaker with ice and shake well. Strain into a chilled martini glass and garnish with the lime wedge. —*Audrey Saunders*

GREEN LANTERN

●STRONG ●SWEET ●TART ●BITTER ●FRUITY ●FLORAL ●SMOKY

The Heirloom

●●●●● | ᵀ | Makes: **1**

Star pastry chef Johnny Iuzzini created this cocktail while bartending at the Manhattan bar PDT. He spritzes the drink with anise hyssop essence (available at *aftelier.com*), which adds a pop of sweet licorice flavor.

7   **Concord grapes or ¾ ounce Concord grape juice**
½   **ounce fresh lime juice**
1½   **ounces Old Tom gin**
½   **ounce Cynar (bitter artichoke aperitif)**
¼   **ounce Strega (saffron-infused liqueur)**
     Ice
2   **spritzes of diluted Aftelier anise hyssop essence or spearmint essence (optional)**

In a cocktail shaker, muddle the grapes with the lime juice. Add the gin, Cynar and Strega; fill the shaker with ice and shake well. Strain into a chilled coupe, then spritz the hyssop essence over the drink. —*Johnny Iuzzini*

Genever Blush

●●●● | ᵀ | Makes: **1**

Nick Kobbernagel Hovind of Ruby in Copenhagen says this aperitif is a good way to sneak Campari into guests' glasses if they are not accustomed to bitter flavors. The genever, a distilled, grain-based spirit that originated in Holland, gives the drink a light malty flavor.

⅔   **ounce genever, preferably Bols**
⅔   **ounce Lillet blanc**
⅔   **ounce Campari**
½   **passion fruit, or ½ ounce passion fruit nectar or juice**
⅓   **ounce gum syrup (simple syrup thickened with gum arabic) or Simple Syrup (p. 22)**
     Ice
6 to 8 passion fruit seeds, for garnish (optional)

In a cocktail shaker, combine the genever, Lillet, Campari, passion fruit and syrup; fill the shaker with ice and shake well. Fine-strain (p. 21) into a chilled coupe and garnish with the passion fruit seeds. —*Nick Kobbernagel Hovind*

The Journalist

● ▢▢ | ♈ | Makes: **1**

This classic drink appears in the 1930 tome *The Savoy Cocktail Book*. Essentially a perfect martini (with equal parts sweet and dry vermouth), The Journalist gets great citrus flavor from lemon juice and Cointreau.

1½ ounces gin, preferably London dry
¼   ounce sweet vermouth
¼   ounce dry vermouth
¼   ounce Cointreau or other triple sec
¼   ounce fresh lemon juice
    Dash of Angostura bitters
    Ice
1   lemon twist, for garnish

In a cocktail shaker, combine the gin, vermouths, Cointreau, lemon juice and bitters; fill the shaker with ice and shake well. Strain into a chilled martini glass and garnish with the lemon twist. *—Classic*

Dalí

●● ▢ | ♈ | Makes: **1**

Cocktail innovator Eben Klemm conceived of the Dalí as a surrealist take on a dirty martini. "The roasted pimiento garnish floats on the drink without its natural protector, the olive," Klemm says. "It looks like one of Dalí's melted clocks."

1   orange wedge
    Sea salt
1½ ounces gin, preferably Plymouth
1   ounce manzanilla sherry
½   ounce Cointreau or other triple sec
2   dashes of orange bitters
    Ice
1   strip of roasted red pepper, for garnish

Moisten one-third of the outer rim of a chilled martini glass with the orange wedge and coat lightly with salt. In a mixing glass, combine the gin, sherry, Cointreau, bitters and a small pinch of salt; fill two-thirds of the mixing glass with ice and stir well. Strain into the prepared martini glass and garnish with the roasted red pepper. *—Eben Klemm*

The Tax Lawyer

1½ ounces genever, preferably Bols
¾ ounce sweet vermouth
¾ ounce dry vermouth
½ teaspoon Fernet-Branca (bitter Italian digestif)
½ teaspoon fresh orange juice
    Ice
 1 orange twist, for garnish

In a mixing glass, combine the genever, vermouths, Fernet and orange juice; fill the glass with ice and stir well. Strain into a chilled coupe and garnish with the orange twist. —*Derek Brown*

●◐○ | ! | Makes: **1**

DC mixologist Derek Brown pays tribute to local restaurateur Mark Kuller, who is also a successful tax lawyer. "He let me sip his pricey wines while I made him drinks," says Brown about their first meetup.

Mediterranean Pink Lady

1½ ounces gin, preferably London dry
½ ounce Cointreau or other triple sec
½ ounce fresh lemon juice
¼ ounce limoncello
¼ ounce Campari
 1 large egg white
    Ice
3 or 4 thin strips of lemon zest, for garnish

In a cocktail shaker, combine all of the ingredients except ice and the garnish and shake vigorously. Fill the shaker with ice and shake again. Strain the drink into a chilled coupe and garnish with the lemon zest. —*Angus Winchester*

●◐○○ | ! | Makes: **1**

Combining limoncello and Campari creates a pretty pink drink that's crisp and citrusy. The shaken egg white gives it a light, frothy topping.

Prior's Fix

●●●● | ❚ | Makes: **1**

Prior's Fix is a twist on the Ramos Gin Fizz, a classic hair-of-the-dog cocktail, according to James Wampler, bartender at Eleanor's in Smyrna, Georgia. "The heavy cream, egg white and citrus— all part of a complete breakfast!" he says.

¾   teaspoon Islay Scotch
2   ounces dry gin, such as No. 209
1   ounce heavy cream
¾   ounce Bénédictine (spiced herbal liqueur)
½   ounce Simple Syrup (p. 22)
½   ounce fresh lemon juice
½   ounce fresh lime juice
1   large egg white
    Ice
2   ounces chilled club soda

Rinse a chilled collins glass with the Scotch; do not pour out. In a cocktail shaker, combine the gin, cream, Bénédictine, Simple Syrup, citrus juices and egg white; shake vigorously. Fill with ice and shake again. Pour into the glass; top with the soda. —*James Wampler*

Violet Fizz

●●● | ❚ | Makes: **1**

Before crème de violette was available in the US, New York City mixologist Eben Freeman used to smuggle the fragrant liqueur from London or Paris in his luggage. When the US began allowing imports in 2007, Freeman says, "It was a real treat to find a bottle in Des Moines!"

2   ounces gin, preferably Plymouth
½   ounce crème de violette
½   ounce fresh lemon juice
½   ounce fresh lime juice
½   ounce half-and-half
¼   ounce Simple Syrup (p. 22)
1   large egg white
    Ice
2   ounces chilled club soda
1   fresh edible violet, for garnish (optional)

In a cocktail shaker, combine all of the ingredients except ice, the club soda and the garnish; shake vigorously. Fill the shaker with ice and shake again. Strain the drink into a chilled highball glass, top with the club soda and garnish. —*Eben Freeman*

Tequila

Trends of the decade ● The margarita endures as the country's most popular tequila cocktail. ● Sipping is in, shooting is out: Premium 100 percent blue agave tequilas inspire connoisseurs to enjoy every drop. ● Tequilas that are 80-plus-proof join the ranks of high-octane spirits like overproof rum and cask-strength whiskey. ● Single-field bottlings from producers like Ocho showcase the *terroir* of Mexican regions. ● Mezcal becomes the darling of mixologists; new bottlings feature over a dozen different species of agave.

STRONG SWEET TART BITTER FRUITY FLORAL SMOKY

L'IL JIG, P. 74

CORTEZ JULEP, P. 74

COLONIA ROMA, P. 76

MANZARITA, P. 76

IN-SANDIARY, P. 77

BATANGA, P. 77

MARIA'S MARGARITA, P. 78

LA ROSITA, P. 80

TOMMY'S MARGAR TA, P. 80

OAXACA OLD-FASHIONED, P. 81

POBLANO ESCOBAR, P. 81

NOUVEAU CARRÉ, P. 82

BOHEMIO, P. 82

PAB'S BUCK, P. 84

AÑEJO MANHATTAN, P. 85

MAGUEY SOUR, P. 85

GRAPES OF WRATH, P. 86

NAKED & FAMOUS, P. 86

L'il Jig

●●●● | ⊤ | Makes: **1**

Philip Ward, the mastermind behind the tequila-focused Mayahuel in Manhattan, named this herb-inflected cocktail after the small jigger that mixologists use to measure their drinks precisely.

3   **Thai basil leaves**
¾   **ounce fresh lime juice**
½   **ounce Simple Syrup (p. 22)**
1½ **ounces blanco tequila**
½   **ounce yellow Chartreuse (spicy herbal liqueur)**
    Ice

In a cocktail shaker, muddle the basil with the lime juice and Simple Syrup. Add the tequila and Chartreuse, fill the shaker with ice and shake well. Fine-strain (p. 21) into a chilled coupe. —*Philip Ward*

Cortez Julep

▮ | Makes: **1**

"The marriage of sherry and tequila might have been the golden discovery Cortez was looking for," says Bobby Heugel of Anvil Bar & Refuge in Houston. The key to the combination in this crushed-ice drink is using a nutty oloroso sherry and a bold tequila, such as 7 Leguas Blanco.

12   **mint leaves, plus 1 mint sprig for garnish**
1¼ **ounces blanco tequila**
½   **ounce oloroso sherry**
½   **ounce Cocchi Americano (fortified, slightly bitter aperitif wine)**
¾   **teaspoon Simple Syrup (p. 22)**
     Dash of Angostura bitters
     Dash of orange bitters
     Crushed ice (p. 21)
1   **blackberry, for garnish**

In a chilled julep cup, muddle the mint leaves. Add the tequila, sherry, Cocchi Americano, Simple Syrup and both bitters; fill with crushed ice and mix by spinning a swizzle stick or bar spoon between your hands. Top with more crushed ice and garnish with the blackberry. Lightly smack (p. 21) the mint sprig over the drink, then add it to the cup as garnish. Serve with a metal spoon-straw. —*Bobby Heugel*

CORTEZ JULEP

Colonia Roma

●●○ | ⧖ | Makes: **1**

Anvil Bar's drinks list says, "Don't know what Branca Menta is? Please, ask your bartender. You're welcome." Branca Menta is a digestif with a strong minty-menthol flavor that people either love or hate.

1½ ounces blanco tequila
1½ ounces dry vermouth
½ ounce yellow Chartreuse (spicy herbal liqueur)
½ ounce Branca Menta
½ ounce fresh lime juice
¾ teaspoon Simple Syrup (p. 22)
   Ice
 1 grapefruit twist, for garnish

In a cocktail shaker, combine all of the ingredients except ice and the garnish; fill the shaker with ice and shake well. Strain into a chilled coupe and garnish with the grapefruit twist. —*Bobby Heugel*

Manzarita

●●●○ | ▮ | Makes: **1**

This tequila smash from Devlin DeVore Kaplan of Jax Fish House & Oyster Bar in Boulder, Colorado, gets its autumnal feel from apple cider ("apple" is *manzana* in Spanish) and cinnamon.

½ lemon, quartered
   Pinch of ground cinnamon
 2 ounces blanco tequila
1½ ounces chilled unsweetened apple cider
 1 ounce St-Germain elderflower liqueur
   Ice
 1 cinnamon stick, for garnish

In a cocktail shaker, muddle the lemon quarters with the ground cinnamon. Add the tequila, apple cider and elderflower liqueur; fill the shaker with ice and shake well. Strain into a chilled, ice-filled rocks glass and garnish with the cinnamon stick. —*Devlin DeVore Kaplan*

In-Sandíary

CHILE SALT
1 **teaspoon ancho chile powder**
1 **teaspoon kosher salt**
1 **teaspoon sugar**

COCKTAIL
1 **lime wedge**
2 **ounces blanco tequila**
2 **ounces watermelon juice**
½ **ounce fresh lime juice**
¼ **ounce Simple Syrup (p. 22)**
   Ice

●●○ | **❙** | Makes: **1**

Joaquín Simó of Manhattan's Pouring Ribbons, and a former *F&W Cocktails* deputy editor, remakes the Mexican street-cart drink *agua fresca de sandía* as a cocktail. The salt and spice in the rim make the watermelon taste even sweeter.

1. Make the chile salt On a small plate, mix the chile powder, salt and sugar.

2. Make the cocktail Moisten the outer rim of a chilled highball glass with the lime; coat lightly with the chile salt. In a shaker, combine the tequila, juices and Simple Syrup; fill with ice and shake well. Fill the glass with ice and strain the drink into the glass. —*Joaquín Simó*

Batanga

1 **lime wedge plus ½ lime**
   Kosher salt
   Ice
1½ **ounces blanco tequila**
3 **ounces chilled Coca-Cola**

●● | **❙** | Makes: **1**

Batanga (Spanish slang for "thick in the middle") was the nickname of a rotund regular at La Capilla bar in Tequila, Mexico, where this drink originated. Meant to be rustic, the cocktail is typically stirred with a steak knife.

Moisten the outer rim of a chilled collins glass with the lime wedge and coat lightly with salt; fill with ice. Add the tequila, squeeze the lime half over the drink and drop it in, then top with the Coca-Cola and stir. —*Don Javier*

Maria's Margarita

●●● | ꭲ | Makes: **6**

Time: **20 min** plus freezing

The cucumber mix in this margarita from Todd Thrasher of Restaurant Eve in Alexandria, Virginia, is used in two ways: It's shaken into the drink as a liquid and as ice cubes. The ice cubes, which are strained out, chill the drink without diluting its cucumber flavor.

SPICE MIX
- 2 **teaspoons superfine sugar**
- 2 **teaspoons cayenne pepper**
- 2 **teaspoons sea salt**

COCKTAIL
- 1 **lime wedge**
- 12 **ounces blanco tequila**
- 6 **ounces Cointreau or other triple sec**
- 6 **ounces Cucumber Mix (below)**
- 12 **Cucumber Ice Cubes (below)**
- 6 **cucumber wheels, for garnish**

1. Make the spice mix On a small plate, combine the sugar, cayenne pepper and salt.

2. Make the cocktail Moisten the outer rims of 6 chilled martini glasses with the lime wedge and coat lightly with the spice mix. In a cocktail shaker, combine the tequila, Cointreau and Cucumber Mix; add the Cucumber Ice Cubes and shake well. Strain into the prepared martini glasses and garnish with the cucumber wheels.

CUCUMBER MIX & CUCUMBER ICE CUBES

In a medium bowl, mix the juice of 2 English cucumbers with 2½ ounces fresh lemon juice, 2½ ounces fresh lime juice, ¾ ounce Simple Syrup (p. 22) and ½ teaspoon salt. Reserve 8 ounces for the drinks; pour the rest into an ice cube tray and freeze. Makes 8 ounces Cucumber Mix and about 1 dozen ice cubes.
—*Todd Thrasher*

MARIA'S MARGARITA
"Vitis" martini glass
by Riedel.

La Rosita

●●● | �

 | Makes: **1**

"La Rosita is a very simple drink that celebrates the flavors of tequila," says Robert Hess. He's a self-taught bar expert and creator of the Chanticleer Society, a website for the cocktail-obsessed.

1½ ounces reposado tequila
½ ounce dry vermouth
½ ounce sweet vermouth
½ ounce Campari
    Dash of Angostura bitters
    Ice

In a mixing glass, combine the tequila, vermouths, Campari and bitters; fill two-thirds of the glass with ice and stir well. Strain into a chilled martini glass. —*Robert Hess*

Tommy's Margarita

●● | ▪ | Makes: **1**

Instead of using citrusy triple sec, Julio Bermejo, owner of Tommy's Mexican Restaurant in San Francisco, prefers to sweeten his margaritas with neutrally flavored agave nectar.

2 ounces reposado tequila
1 ounce fresh lime juice
1 ounce agave syrup (1 tablespoon agave nectar mixed with 1 tablespoon water)
    Ice

In a cocktail shaker, combine the tequila, lime juice and agave syrup; fill the shaker with ice and shake well. Strain into a chilled, ice-filled double rocks glass. —*Julio Bermejo*

Oaxaca Old-Fashioned

1½ ounces reposado tequila
½ ounce mezcal
2 dashes of Angostura bitters
1 teaspoon agave nectar
   Ice
1 orange twist, flamed (p. 20),
   for garnish

In a mixing glass, combine the tequila, mezcal, bitters and agave nectar; fill the glass with ice and stir well. Strain into a chilled, ice-filled double rocks glass and garnish with the flamed orange twist. —*Philip Ward*

●●● | ▮ | Makes: **1**

"Most tequila in the US is only 80 proof, and I wanted more oomph! I discovered it in mezcal," says New York City mixologist Philip Ward. The combination of tequila and mezcal here, he says, "is like putting tequila on steroids."

Poblano Escobar

Four ¼-inch-thick rings of poblano chile
Four 1-inch chunks of fresh pineapple
   Small pinch of cumin
1 ounce reposado tequila, preferably 7 Leguas
1 ounce mezcal
1 ounce fresh lemon juice
¾ ounce triple sec, preferably Combier
½ ounce agave nectar
   Ice
1 orange wheel, for garnish

In a cocktail shaker, muddle 3 of the chile rings with the pineapple and cumin. Add the tequila, mezcal, lemon juice, triple sec and agave nectar; fill the shaker with ice and shake well. Fine-strain (p. 21) into a chilled, ice-filled rocks glass and garnish with the orange wheel and remaining chile ring. —*Julian Cox*

●●●● | ▮ | Makes: **1**

Cumin may seem unusual in a cocktail, but L.A. mixology consultant Julian Cox adds a small pinch here. It enhances the smokiness of mezcal while keeping the sweetness of the pineapple and triple sec in check.

Nouveau Carré

●● | ⊤ | Makes: **1**

Created in the wake of Hurricane Katrina by Jonny Raglin when he was at Absinthe in San Francisco, the Nouveau Carré is a riff on the classic New Orleans cocktail Vieux Carré.

1½ ounces añejo tequila
¾ ounce Lillet blanc
½ ounce Bénédictine (spiced herbal liqueur)
5 dashes of Peychaud's bitters
   Ice
1 lemon twist, for garnish

In a mixing glass, combine the tequila, Lillet, Bénédictine and bitters; fill the glass with ice and stir well. Strain into a chilled coupe and garnish with the lemon twist. —*Jonny Raglin*

Bohemio

●●●● | ▪ | Makes: **1**

Mixologist Eben Freeman makes this drink with *naranja agria*, a mouth-puckering sour orange found in Dominican markets near his home in Harlem. For those who don't live close to a Dominican greengrocer, he suggests combining equal parts orange and lemon juice.

2 ounces reposado tequila
½ ounce Becherovka (bittersweet liqueur)
½ ounce fresh lemon juice
½ ounce fresh orange juice
½ ounce Simple Syrup (p. 22)
¼ ounce mezcal
   Ice
1 orange twist, flamed (p. 20), for garnish

In a cocktail shaker, combine the tequila, Becherovka, citrus juices, Simple Syrup and mezcal; fill the shaker with ice and shake well. Strain into a chilled, ice-filled rocks glass and garnish with the flamed orange twist. —*Eben Freeman*

BOHEMIO
"Culbuto" decanter
by Moser.

Pab's Buck

●●● | ▍ | Makes: **1**

This sweet-tart strawberry cocktail is an homage from François Vera of Pour Vous in Los Angeles to his grandfather Pablo Vera, who made a similar drink at his bar in São Paulo, Brazil.

4 **ounces strawberries, plus 1 strawberry wrapped in a lime wheel for garnish**

2 **tablespoons plus 2 teaspoons superfine sugar**

2 **ounces añejo tequila**

½ **ounce triple sec, preferably Combier**

½ **ounce fresh lime juice**

4 **dashes of rhubarb bitters**

¾ **teaspoon apple drinking vinegar, such as Bragg**
   Pinch of kosher salt
   Ice

2 **ounces chilled club soda**

In a blender, puree the 4 ounces of strawberries and the sugar. In a cocktail shaker, combine ¾ ounce of the strawberry puree (reserve the rest for another use) with the tequila, triple sec, lime juice, bitters, vinegar and salt; fill the shaker with ice and shake well. Strain into a chilled, ice-filled collins glass, stir in the soda and garnish with the strawberry wrapped in a lime wheel. —*François Vera*

Añejo Manhattan

- 2 **ounces añejo tequila**
- ½ **ounce sweet vermouth**
- ¼ **ounce Licor 43 (citrus-and-vanilla-flavored Spanish liqueur)**
- **Dash of Angostura bitters**
- **Dash of orange bitters**
- **Ice**
- 1 **fresh cherry, for garnish**

In a mixing glass, combine the tequila, vermouth, Licor 43 and both bitters; fill two-thirds of the glass with ice and stir well. Strain into a chilled martini glass and garnish with the cherry. —*Ryan Magarian*

 | ¥ | Makes: **1**

Ryan Magarian, co-owner of Oven and Shaker in Portland, Oregon, likes to garnish the Añejo Manhattan with a snack: a tequila-marinated dried cherry wrapped in a slice of mole-spiced salami.

Maguey Sour

- 2 **ounces mezcal**
- ¾ **ounce fresh lemon juice**
- ½ **ounce Bénédictine (spiced herbal liqueur)**
- ½ **ounce orgeat (almond-flavored syrup)**
- ½ **large egg white**
- **Ice**
- **Pinch of freshly grated nutmeg and 1 orange twist, for garnish**

In a cocktail shaker, combine the mezcal, lemon juice, Bénédictine, orgeat and egg white and shake vigorously; fill the shaker with ice and shake again. Strain into a chilled, ice-filled rocks glass and garnish with the grated nutmeg and orange twist. —*Jacques Bezuidenhout*

 | ■ | Makes: **1**
📷 Cover

Jacques Bezuidenhout prefers Del Maguey, one of his favorite mezcals, for this drink. (Maguey is another name for agave.) The cocktail is his take on a classic sour, enhanced with a pleasing nutti-ness from almond syrup.

Grapes of Wrath

●●●● | ❚ | Makes: **1**

Leo Robitschek, bar director at Eleven Madison Park and The NoMad Hotel in New York City, showcases fragrant Concord grapes in this cocktail. Barolo Chinato, a spiced fortified red wine, intensifies the drink's grapey flavor.

1   ounce mezcal
¾   ounce fino sherry
¾   ounce Barolo Chinato
¾   ounce fresh lemon juice
½   ounce Vanilla Simple Syrup (p. 22)
     Crushed ice (p. 21)
15   Concord grapes
¼   ounce Simple Syrup (p. 22)

In a chilled highball glass, combine the mezcal, sherry, Barolo Chinato, lemon juice and Vanilla Simple Syrup. Fill the glass with crushed ice and mix by spinning a swizzle stick or bar spoon between your hands. In a mixing glass, muddle the grapes with the Simple Syrup and pour over the drink. —*Leo Robitschek*

Naked & Famous

●●●●● | ⊤ | Makes: **1**

"A big, aggressively smoky and funky mezcal is key here," says New York City mixologist Joaquín Simó. He recommends Del Maguey's Chichicapa mezcal.

¾   ounce mezcal
¾   ounce yellow Chartreuse
     (spicy herbal liqueur)
¾   ounce Aperol
¾   ounce fresh lime juice
     Ice

In a cocktail shaker, combine the mezcal, Chartreuse, Aperol and lime juice; fill the shaker with ice and shake well. Strain into a chilled coupe. —*Joaquín Simó*

NAKED & FAMOUS

Rum

Trends of the decade ● Twists on the classic rum cocktail daiquiri generate excitement about other sugarcane spirits: cachaça and rhum agricole. ● The mojito challenges the margarita as the most popular cocktail in America–and loses! (Bartenders don't love this muddling-intensive drink.) ● The revival of forgotten classics brings back vintage rums and rum-based liqueurs (British Navy rum, Velvet Falernum and pimento dram). ● Tiki drinks and lounges make an epic comeback, boosted by tiki book author Jeff Berry and the preponderance of freshly squeezed juice at bars.

STRONG SWEET TART BITTER FRUITY FLORAL SMOKY

EWING NO. 33, P. 90
RUM RIVER MYSTIC, P. 90
GOLDEN AGE, P. 92
STIRRED SLING, P. 92
AVOCADO DAIQUIRI, P. 93
LA FLORIDITA, P. 93
FOG CUTTER, P. 94
DOLORES PARK SWIZZLE, P. 94
CAPRESE DAIQUIRI, P. 96
ESPRESSO BONGO, P. 96
AUTUMN DAIQUIRI, P. 97
CABLE CAR, P. 97
STONE WALL, P. 98
THAI BOXER, P. 98
CAIPIRINHA MANCHADA, P. 100
MEDFORD WARMER, P. 101

Ewing No. 33

●●◐ | ⊤ | Makes: **1**

Basketball great Patrick Ewing grew up within blocks of Green Street, Dylan Black's cocktail-focused restaurant in Cambridge, Massachusetts. Black uses Jamaican rum here to honor Ewing's birthplace, Kingston.

¼ ounce pastis
2 ounces amber rum
½ ounce Fernet-Branca (bitter Italian digestif)
¼ ounce Spiced Brown Sugar Syrup (below)
   Dash of Angostura bitters
   Ice
1 lime wedge, for garnish

Rinse a chilled coupe with the pastis; pour out the excess. In a mixing glass, combine the rum, Fernet, syrup and bitters; fill with ice and stir well. Strain into the prepared coupe and garnish.

SPICED BROWN SUGAR SYRUP
In a saucepan, bring 8 ounces water to a boil with 1 cup dark brown sugar, 2 allspice berries and 1 star anise pod. Simmer over moderate heat for 5 minutes. Let cool, strain into an airtight container and refrigerate up to 2 weeks. Makes about 12 ounces. —*Dylan Black*

Rum River Mystic

●●◐ | ■ | Makes: **1**

📷 p. 201

In Haiti, voodoo priests soak the ground with the best golden Barbancourt rum to summon the spirits of the dead. Here, Paul McGee of Chicago's Bub City combines Barbancourt with Trinidadian rum.

1 ounce amber Haitian rum
1 ounce Trinidadian rum, preferably The Scarlet Ibis
¾ ounce Byrrh Grand Quinquina (slightly bitter aperitif wine)
¼ ounce Bénédictine (spiced herbal liqueur)
2 dashes of Angostura bitters
   Ice, plus 1 large ice cube (p. 21) for serving
1 orange twist, for garnish

In a mixing glass, combine all of the ingredients except ice and the garnish; fill with ice and stir well. Strain into a chilled double rocks glass over the large ice cube and garnish with the orange twist. —*Paul McGee*

EWING NO. 33

Golden Age

●●○ | ▮ | Makes: **1**

When Toby Maloney
concocted this drink for
The Violet Hour in
Chicago, he wanted it to
be a study in contrasts.
He balances tart lemon
juice with sweet cherry
liqueur and vanilla-
inflected rum with
plenty of bitters.

  2 **ounces amber rum**
  ¾ **ounce fresh lemon juice**
  ½ **ounce Heering cherry liqueur**
  ½ **ounce Simple Syrup (p. 22)**
  1 **large egg yolk**
  5 **dashes of lemon bitters**
    Ice cubes, plus crushed ice (p. 21) for serving
  1 **lemon wheel skewered on a pick with
    1 maraschino cherry, for garnish**

In a cocktail shaker, combine all of the ingredients
except ice and the garnish; shake vigorously. Fill the
shaker with ice cubes and shake again. Strain into
a chilled, crushed-ice-filled highball glass and garnish
with the lemon wheel and cherry. —*Toby Maloney*

Stirred Sling

●●○○ | ▼ | Makes: **1**

Julie Reiner, co-owner
of Flatiron Lounge
in Manhattan, created
this drink when she
was challenged to rein-
vent the Singapore
Sling for *F&W Cocktails*.
To preserve the tropical
flavors while omitting
the juice, Reiner uses
rums with hints of
berries and pineapple.

  1 **ounce aged Jamaican rum, preferably Appleton
Estate Reserve**
  1 **ounce dark rum, preferably Zafra**
  ½ **teaspoon Bénédictine (spiced herbal liqueur)**
  ½ **teaspoon maraschino liqueur**
  ½ **teaspoon Grand Marnier**
  2 **dashes of orange bitters**
    Ice
  1 **lime twist, for garnish**

In a mixing glass, combine all of the ingredients
except ice and the garnish; fill the glass with
ice and stir well. Strain into a chilled coupe and
garnish with the lime twist. —*Julie Reiner*

Avocado Daiquiri

- 2   **ounces white rum**
- 2   **ounces dark rum**
- 2   **ounces Simple Syrup (p. 22)**
- 1   **ounce fresh lemon juice**
- ¼   **Hass avocado, peeled and sliced**
- 1½ **teaspoons half-and-half**
- 1   **cup crushed ice (p. 21)**

In a blender, combine all of the ingredients. Blend until the drink is completely smooth, then pour into a chilled wineglass. —*Lucy Brennan*

 | ♟ | Makes: **1**

"This drink has gone from ugly duckling to swan," says Lucy Brennan. It took her years to perfect this banana daiquiri revamp; it's now a best seller at Mint/820, her restaurant and bar in Portland, Oregon.

La Floridita

- 2   **ounces white rum**
- ¾   **ounce fresh lime juice**
- ½   **ounce Punt e Mes or other sweet vermouth**
- ½   **ounce white crème de cacao**
- ½   **teaspoon grenadine, preferably homemade (p. 22)**
-     **Ice**
- 1   **lime wheel, for garnish**

In a cocktail shaker, combine the rum, lime juice, vermouth, crème de cacao and grenadine; fill the shaker with ice and shake well. Strain into a chilled coupe and garnish with the lime wheel. —*Classic*

●●● | ☍ | Makes: **1**

Based on a drink once served at the famous Havana bar Floridita, this updated version is served straight up, with a little more rum.

Fog Cutter

●● | ❙ | Makes: **1**

The Fog Cutter is a classic concoction from the legendary Victor "Trader Vic" Bergeron. Martin Cate, owner of Smuggler's Cove in San Francisco, loves it so much that he not only serves the tiki drink at his bar, he's also the registered owner of California license plate FGCUTTR.

2	ounces fresh orange juice
1½	ounces white rum
1	ounce fresh lemon juice
½	ounce gin
½	ounce brandy
½	ounce orgeat (almond-flavored syrup)
	Ice
½	ounce amontillado sherry
1	mint sprig, for garnish

In a shaker, combine the orange juice, rum, lemon juice, gin, brandy and orgeat; fill with ice and shake well. Strain into a chilled, ice-filled highball glass; float the sherry on top, slowly pouring it over the back of a bar spoon. Garnish with the mint sprig. —*Martin Cate*

Dolores Park Swizzle

●●● | ❙ | Makes: **1**

Thad Vogler, owner of San Francisco's Bar Agricole, created this variation on the classic Queen's Park Swizzle. Aromatic French West Indian rhum agricole stands in for the standard Demerara rum; cane syrup and maraschino liqueur add richness.

2	ounces white rhum agricole
1	ounce fresh lime juice
½	ounce cane syrup (see Note)
¼	ounce maraschino liqueur
½	teaspoon absinthe
	Crushed ice (p. 21) or pebble ice (slightly larger and more rounded than crushed ice)
4	dashes of Peychaud's bitters and 1 or 2 mint sprigs, for garnish

In a chilled collins glass, combine the rhum agricole, lime juice, cane syrup, maraschino liqueur and absinthe. Add crushed ice and spin a swizzle stick or bar spoon between your hands to mix the drink; add more crushed ice. Top with the bitters and mint. —*Thad Vogler*

Note Sweet, thick cane syrup is available at Whole Foods and *cocktailkingdom.com*.

**DOLORES PARK
SWIZZLE**
Straw by Glass Dharma.

Caprese Daiquiri

●● | 🍸 | Makes: **1**

Mathias Simonis of Trick Dog in San Francisco once tasted a chicken Caesar cocktail at a mixology seminar. Inspired to reinvent his own favorite salad, he created this savory Caprese Daiquiri, which can include fun garnishes like olives and pickled peppers.

4 cherry tomatoes
2 basil leaves
¾ teaspoon balsamic vinegar
      Pinch each of salt and freshly ground pepper
2 ounces white rum
¾ ounce Simple Syrup (p. 22)
¾ ounce fresh lime juice
      Ice
      Herbed olive oil and 1 mini mozzarella ball skewered on a pick with 1 cherry tomato and 1 basil leaf, for garnish

In a cocktail shaker, muddle the 4 cherry tomatoes with the 2 basil leaves, vinegar, salt and pepper. Add the rum, Simple Syrup and lime juice, fill the shaker with ice and shake well. Fine-strain (p. 21) into a chilled coupe and garnish with the olive oil, mozzarella ball, cherry tomato and basil leaf. —*Mathias Simonis*

Espresso Bongo

●●●● | ▮ | Makes: **1**

Jeff Berry, author of *Beachbum Berry Remixed: A Gallery of Tiki Drinks*, is one of the world's leading rum experts. Here, he uses his extensive tiki expertise to concoct a tropical rum drink with chilled espresso.

2 ounces amber rum, preferably Barbados
¾ ounce Simple Syrup (p. 22)
½ ounce fresh lime juice
½ ounce fresh orange juice
½ ounce chilled passion fruit nectar or juice
½ ounce chilled brewed espresso
¼ ounce chilled unsweetened pineapple juice
      Ice

In a cocktail shaker, combine all of the ingredients, fill with ice and shake well. Pour—don't strain—into a chilled double rocks glass. —*Jeff Berry*

Autumn Daiquiri

2 ounces aged or spiced rum
¾ ounce fresh lime juice
½ ounce chilled unsweetened pineapple juice
¼ ounce Rich Simple Syrup (p. 22)
¼ ounce Cinnamon Syrup (below)
Dash of Angostura bitters
Ice

In a cocktail shaker, combine all of the ingredients, fill with ice and shake well. Strain into a chilled coupe.

CINNAMON SYRUP

In a small saucepan, bring 8 ounces water to a boil with 1 cup sugar and 6 medium cinnamon sticks broken into pieces. Simmer over moderate heat for 2 minutes, stirring to dissolve the sugar. Let the syrup cool, cover and let stand for 4 hours. Strain the syrup into a jar, cover and refrigerate for up to 1 month. Makes about 12 ounces. —*Joaquín Simó*

●●● | Ｙ | Makes: **1**
Time: **10 min** plus steeping

Originally from Cuba, the daiquiri is usually a warm-weather cocktail. This version from Joaquín Simó of Pouring Ribbons in New York City features spiced flavors that are perfect for cooler months. According to Simó, though, the drink "remains true to its daiquiri roots: tart and refreshing."

Cable Car

1 lemon wedge and superfine sugar
2 ounces spiced rum
1 ounce fresh lemon juice
¾ ounce orange curaçao
Ice
1 orange twist, for garnish

Moisten the outer rim of a chilled martini glass with the lemon wedge and coat lightly with sugar. In a cocktail shaker, combine the rum, lemon juice and curaçao; fill the shaker with ice and shake well. Strain into the prepared martini glass and garnish with the twist. —*Tony Abou-Ganim*

●●● | Ｙ | Makes: **1**

Mixology consultant Tony Abou-Ganim created the Cable Car in 1996 for Harry Denton's Starlight Room, located "between the stars and the cable cars" (according to the slogan) on the top floor of the Sir Francis Drake Hotel in San Francisco.

Stone Wall

●● | ■ | Makes: **1**

According to legendary mixologist Dale DeGroff, the Stone Wall may have been America's first highball, consisting simply of a spirit topped with cider. DeGroff's more refined interpretation adds fresh ginger and ginger beer for a spicy kick.

**One 1-inch piece of fresh ginger,
    peeled and thinly sliced**
1½ teaspoons Simple Syrup (p. 22)
1½ ounces aged rum
1½ ounces chilled unsweetened apple cider
    Ice
1½ ounces chilled ginger beer
  1 lime wedge and 1 apple slice, for garnish

In a cocktail shaker, muddle the ginger with the Simple Syrup. Add the rum and cider, fill the shaker with ice and shake well. Strain into a chilled, ice-filled rocks glass, stir in the ginger beer and garnish with the lime wedge and apple slice. —*Dale DeGroff*

Thai Boxer

●● | ▌ | Makes: **1**

After a backpacking trip though Thailand, Scott Beattie, a partner at Goose & Gander in Napa Valley, began experimenting with Thai herbs. He came up with the Thai Boxer, so named because it "packs a punch."

10 Thai basil leaves, plus 1 Thai basil sprig for garnish
10 mint leaves
10 cilantro leaves
½ ounce Simple Syrup (p. 22)
**1½ ounces vanilla rum, preferably
    Charbay Tahitian**
½ ounce unsweetened coconut milk
½ ounce fresh lime juice
    Ice
  1 ounce chilled ginger beer

In a cocktail shaker, muddle the Thai basil leaves with the mint, cilantro and Simple Syrup. Add the rum, coconut milk and lime juice, fill the shaker with ice and shake well. Strain the drink into a chilled, ice-filled collins glass and stir in the ginger beer. Garnish with the Thai basil sprig. —*Scott Beattie*

STONE WALL
"Bar" glass by Moser;
"Orb" cocktail shaker
by Crate & Barrel.

Caipirinha Manchada

Greg Hoitsma of
Andina in Portland,
Oregon, transforms the
caipirinha (a Brazilian
lime cocktail) with
fruity homemade hibis-
cus *agua fresca.*
The name Caipirinha
Manchada, which
means "stained caipi-
rinha," refers to the
way the hibiscus *agua
fresca* tinges the
limes with crimson.

½   lime, cut into 6 pieces
¾   ounce Simple Syrup (p. 22)
1½ ounces cachaça
 1 cup ice
½   ounce Hibiscus Agua Fresca
    (below)

In a cocktail shaker, muddle the lime pieces with
the Simple Syrup. Add the cachaça and ice; shake well.
Pour the drink into a chilled rocks glass and float the
Hibiscus Agua Fresca on top, slowly pouring it over
the back of a bar spoon near the surface of the drink.

HIBISCUS AGUA FRESCA

In a small heatproof bowl, steep 1 hibiscus tea bag
in 8 ounces boiling water for 3 minutes. Remove
the tea bag. Add 8 black peppercorns, ½ teaspoon
cardamom, ¼ teaspoon allspice, ¼ teaspoon
cinnamon and ¼ teaspoon cloves. Let cool. Strain the
Hibiscus Agua Fresca through a coffee filter into
an airtight container and refrigerate for up to 1 week.
Makes 8 ounces. —*Greg Hoitsma*

Medford Warmer

  1 clove-studded lemon wheel

4½ ounces hot water

  2 ounces aged Trinidadian rum,
     preferably Angostura 1919

  ¾ ounce Apple Juice Reduction
     (below)

  ½ ounce dark crème de cacao, preferably
     Tempus Fugit

     Dash of Angostura bitters

Place the clove-studded lemon wheel in a warmed
mug or heatproof glass. Add the hot water, rum,
Apple Juice Reduction, crème de cacao and bitters
and stir well.

APPLE JUICE REDUCTION

In a small saucepan, simmer 2 cups unfiltered apple
juice over moderate heat until reduced to ½ cup.
Let cool, then pour into a jar and refrigerate for up
to 2 weeks. Makes 4 ounces. —*Jon Santer*

 ●●● | ▶ | Makes: **1**

Hot toddies are mixed
with hot water, which
can make the drink
taste diluted and weak.
Jon Santer of Prize-
fighter in Emeryville,
California, amps up the
flavor of his Medford
Warmer with a simple
apple juice reduction.

Whiskey

Trends of the decade ● Limited-release bourbons, such as Pappy Van Winkle, draw intense fans. ● Craft distillers make white (unaged) whiskey, a.k.a. moonshine. ● The fervor to prepare historically accurate recipes creates a demand for American rye that producers struggle to keep up with. ● Smoky peated single malts and blends become fashionable among Scotch lovers. ● More Japanese whiskies are exported to America, vying with Scotch for medals and prestige.

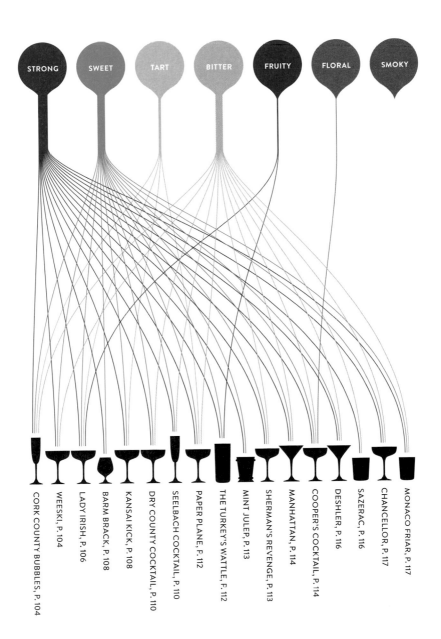

STRONG SWEET TART BITTER FRUITY FLORAL SMOKY

CORK COUNTY BUBBLES, P. 104
WEESKI, P. 104
LADY IRISH, P. 106
BARM BRACK, P. 108
KANSAI KICK, P. 108
DRY COUNTY COCKTAIL, P. 110
SEELBACH COCKTAIL, P. 110
PAPER PLANE, P. 112
THE TURKEY'S WATTLE, F. 112
MINT JULEP, P. 113
SHERMAN'S REVENGE, P. 113
MANHATTAN, P. 114
COOPER'S COCKTAIL, P. 114
DESHLER, P. 116
SAZERAC, P. 116
CHANCELLOR, P. 117
MONACO FRIAR, P. 117

Cork County Bubbles

●●○○ | ! | Makes: **1**

L.A. mixologist John Coltharp likes making this Champagne cocktail with Jameson 12-year Irish whiskey (distilled in County Cork). Because the drink is citrusy, a bright, fruity Champagne works best.

1 **ounce Irish whiskey**
½ **ounce fresh lemon juice**
¼ **ounce yellow Chartreuse (spicy herbal liqueur)**
¼ **ounce Honey Syrup (p. 22)**
   Ice
1 **ounce chilled Champagne**
1 **lemon twist, for garnish**

In a cocktail shaker, combine the whiskey, lemon juice, Chartreuse and Honey Syrup; fill the shaker with ice and shake well. Strain into a chilled flute, stir in the chilled Champagne and garnish with the lemon twist. —*John Coltharp*

Weeski

●●● | ♈ | Makes: **1**

Cocktail historian David Wondrich invented this drink out of desperation when he wanted a Manhattan but had neither rye nor red vermouth in the house. "The Lillet has the sweetness of a red vermouth," Wondrich says, "but it's much gentler."

2 **ounces Irish whiskey**
1 **ounce Lillet blanc**
¾ **ounce Cointreau or other triple sec**
2 **dashes of orange bitters**
   Ice
1 **orange twist, for garnish**

In a mixing glass, combine the whiskey, Lillet, Cointreau and bitters; fill the glass with ice and stir well. Strain into a chilled coupe and garnish with the orange twist. —*David Wondrich*

WEESKI
Bitters bottle by Yarai
from Umami Mart.

Lady Irish

●●●● | ▽ | Makes: **1**

Time: **10 min** plus overnight standing for the syrup

Jack McGarry, managing partner of Manhattan's Dead Rabbit, mixes this tart, food-friendly Champagne cocktail with Bushmills Black Bush, a nutty Irish whiskey. His partner at the Dead Rabbit, Sean Muldoon, likes drinking the cocktail with shellfish, especially shrimp, lobster or crab.

²/₃ ounce Irish whiskey, preferably Bushmills Black Bush

²/₃ ounce oloroso sherry

½ ounce Red Currant Syrup (below) or grenadine, preferably homemade (p. 22)

⅓ ounce fresh lemon juice

1 teaspoon cane syrup (see Note) or Rich Simple Syrup (p. 22)
   Ice

1²/₃ ounces chilled Champagne
   Small bunch of red currants, for garnish (optional)

In a cocktail shaker, combine the whiskey, sherry, Red Currant Syrup, lemon juice and cane syrup; fill the shaker with ice and shake well. Strain the drink into a chilled coupe and stir in the Champagne. Garnish with the currants.

NOTE Sweet, thick cane syrup is available at Whole Foods and *cocktailkingdom.com*.

RED CURRANT SYRUP

In a heatproof bowl, muddle 1 cup stemmed fresh red currants, cover and let stand at room temperature overnight. Add 1¼ cups superfine sugar and 7 ounces boiling water, stir and let cool completely. Strain the syrup into a jar, cover and refrigerate for up to 1 week. Makes about 12 ounces. *—Jack McGarry*

LADY IRISH

Barm Brack

●● | ♥ | Makes: **1**

Time: **10 min** plus simmering and cooling the syrup

Barm brack is an Irish Halloween bread studded with raisins and currants. Traditionally, various objects—a coin, a ring, a pea—were baked inside the loaf as a kind of fortune-telling game. Belfast native Jack McGarry reimagines the bread as a creamy, spiced flip-style cocktail.

  2 **ounces single-malt Irish whiskey**
  ½ **teaspoon St. Elizabeth allspice dram (rum-based allspice liqueur)**
 ⅔ **ounce Toasted-Raisin Syrup (below)**
  ½ **ounce heavy cream**
  1 **large egg yolk**
     Pinch of salt
     Ice
     Pinch of freshly grated nutmeg, for garnish

In a cocktail shaker, combine the whiskey, allspice dram, syrup, cream, egg yolk and salt; shake vigorously. Fill with ice and shake again. Strain into a chilled snifter and garnish with the nutmeg.

TOASTED-RAISIN SYRUP

In a saucepan, toast 1 cup raisins over moderate heat until fragrant, about 5 minutes. Add 1¼ cups superfine sugar and 7 ounces hot water and simmer for 10 minutes. Let cool completely, then strain into a jar, cover and refrigerate for up to 1 month. Makes about 9 ounces. —*Jack McGarry*

Kansai Kick

●●● | ▼ | Makes: **1**

John deBary, bar director for the Momofuku restaurant group, makes this zippy drink with Scotch-like Yamazaki whisky, which is from the Kansai region of Japan.

1½ **ounces Japanese whisky, preferably Yamazaki 12-year-old**
 ¾ **ounce Sercial Madeira**
 ¾ **ounce fresh lime juice**
     Scant ½ ounce orgeat (almond-flavored syrup)
     Ice

In a cocktail shaker, combine the whisky, Madeira, lime juice and orgeat; fill the shaker with ice and shake well. Strain into a chilled coupe. —*John deBary*

Dry County Cocktail

● ● ● | ⊤ | Makes: **1**
Time: **10 min** plus
overnight steeping
for the syrup

This Manhattan varia-
tion is from Jonny
Raglin of Comstock
Saloon in San Francisco.
He likes to make
it with George Dickel
No. 12, which is dis-
tilled in the dry county
of Coffee, Tennessee.

2 ounces Tennessee whiskey
¾ ounce dry vermouth
½ ounce Ginger Syrup (below)
   Dash of lemon bitters
   Ice
1 lemon twist, for garnish

In a mixing glass, combine the whiskey, vermouth,
Ginger Syrup and bitters; fill the glass with ice and
stir well. Strain into a chilled coupe and garnish with
the lemon twist.

GINGER SYRUP

Peel and dice 1 ounce fresh ginger. In a small
saucepan, bring 6 ounces Simple Syrup (p. 22) to a
boil. Remove from the heat and add the ginger. Let
cool, then refrigerate overnight. Strain into an airtight
container and refrigerate for up to 3 weeks. Makes
6 ounces. —Jonny Raglin

Seelbach Cocktail

● ● ● | ! | Makes: **1**

According to legend,
this intriguingly bitter
drink was born in
1917 when a bartender
at the Seelbach Hotel
in Louisville, Kentucky,
accidentally poured
Champagne into
a guest's Manhattan.

1 ounce bourbon
½ ounce Cointreau or other triple sec
7 dashes of Angostura bitters
7 dashes of Peychaud's bitters
   Ice
5 ounces chilled Champagne
1 orange twist, for garnish

In a mixing glass, combine the bourbon, Cointreau
and both bitters; fill two-thirds of the glass with ice
and stir well. Strain into a chilled flute, stir in the
Champagne and garnish with the twist. —Adam Seger

SEELBACH
COCKTAIL

Paper Plane

●●○○ | ▼ | Makes: **1**

"This drink is delicious,"
says Sam Ross, a
co-owner of Attaboy
in New York City. "But
what makes it popular
is that it has no fancy
syrups; all the ingredients can be found in
any well-stocked bar."

¾   ounce bourbon
¾   ounce Nonino Quintessentia amaro
    (bittersweet Italian liqueur)
¾   ounce Aperol
¾   ounce fresh lemon juice
    Ice

In a cocktail shaker, combine the bourbon, amaro,
Aperol and lemon juice; fill the shaker with ice and
shake well. Strain into a chilled coupe. —*Sam Ross*

The Turkey's Wattle

●●● | ▮ | Makes: **1**

The Turkey's Wattle is
from Bill Norris, beverage director of the
Midnight Cowboy and
Alamo Drafthouse in
Austin. Inspired by a
punch that he made for
Thanksgiving one year,
the rye cocktail has the
flavors of fall: apple
cider, ginger beer and a
bit of allspice liqueur.

2½ ounces rye whiskey, preferably
    Wild Turkey Rye 101 proof
 1 ounce chilled unsweetened apple cider
½   ounce Simple Syrup (p. 22)
¾   teaspoon St. Elizabeth allspice dram
    (rum-based allspice liqueur)
Two 6-inch strips of orange zest
    Ice
 2 ounces chilled ginger beer

In a cocktail shaker, combine the whiskey, apple
cider, Simple Syrup, allspice dram and 1 of the orange
zest strips; fill the shaker with ice and shake well.
Strain into a chilled, ice-filled collins glass, stir in the
ginger beer and garnish with the remaining strip of
orange zest. —*Bill Norris*

Mint Julep

8 mint leaves, plus mint sprigs for garnish
½ ounce Simple Syrup (p. 22)
2 ounces bourbon, preferably overproof
    Crushed ice (p. 21)

In a chilled julep cup, gently muddle the mint leaves
with the Simple Syrup. Add the bourbon and fill the
glass with crushed ice. Spin a swizzle stick or bar
spoon between your hands to mix the drink. Top with
more crushed ice and garnish with the mint sprigs.
—Chris McMillian

●● | ▮ | Makes: 1

Chris McMillian of
Kingfish in New
Orleans is said to make
the city's best mint
julep. His secret:
muddling the mint
gently; pounding
too hard will extract
bitter elements.

Sherman's Revenge

2½ ounces rye whiskey
1 ounce cream sherry
    Dash of orange bitters
3 orange twists, flamed (p. 20),
    for garnish
    Ice

In a mixing glass, combine the whiskey, sherry
and bitters. Flame 2 orange twists over the glass,
then drop them in. Fill the glass with ice and
stir well. Strain into a chilled coupe. Flame the
remaining twist over the drink, then drop it in.
—Eric Simpkins

●●● | ▼ | Makes: 1

After a stint in New
York City, Eric Simpkins
returned home to
invigorate the Atlanta
cocktail scene and is
now at The Lawrence.
The flaming orange
twist is a showy bar-
tender's trick that has
a practical function
here: caramelizing the
essential oils in the peel.

Manhattan

●●● | ⅋ | Makes: **1**

When making a Manhattan, purists insist on the classic rye, which has a spicy bite, while others prefer their favorite bourbon.

2½ **ounces bourbon or rye whiskey**
 1 **ounce sweet vermouth**
 2 **dashes of Angostura bitters**
   Ice
 1 **orange twist, for garnish**

In a mixing glass, combine the bourbon, vermouth and bitters; fill the glass with ice and stir well. Strain into a chilled martini glass and garnish with the orange twist. —*Classic*

Cooper's Cocktail

●●●● | ⅋ | Makes: **1**

This drink from Seattle mixologist Jamie Boudreau honors Rob Cooper, the founder of St-Germain elderflower liqueur. For the best elderflower flavor, workers at St-Germain handpick the blossoms in the French Alps, then bike over to the distillery right away.

 2 **ounces rye whiskey**
 ¾ **ounce St-Germain elderflower liqueur**
 ¼ **ounce Fernet-Branca (bitter Italian digestif)**
   Ice
 1 **spiral-cut orange twist (p. 20), for garnish**

In a mixing glass, combine the whiskey, St-Germain and Fernet-Branca; fill the glass with ice and stir well. Strain into a chilled coupe and garnish with the orange twist. —*Jamie Boudreau*

COOPER'S COCKTAIL
"Eleanor" Champagne
coupe by William Yeoward.

Deshler

●●● | ☐ | Makes: **1**

The Deshler is a World War I–era cocktail that's said to be named for lightweight boxer Dave Deshler. He had a 14-year career of nearly the same number of wins, losses and draws.

1½ ounces rye whiskey
1½ ounces Dubonnet rouge (wine-based aperitif)
  1 ounce triple sec
  4 dashes of Angostura bitters
     Ice

In a mixing glass, combine the rye, Dubonnet, triple sec and bitters; fill two-thirds of the glass with ice and stir well. Strain into a chilled martini glass. —*Murray Stenson*

Sazerac

●● | ▪ | Makes: **1**

Mike Ryan of Chicago's Sable Kitchen & Bar recalls his first time making a Sazerac. "It was an undrinkable mess; the poor customer was very kind and returned it gently," Ryan says. "That night I went through a bottle of rye trying to nail the drink the way it's presented here."

¼ ounce absinthe
  2 ounces bonded rye whiskey, preferably Rittenhouse 100
½ teaspoon Rich Simple Syrup (p. 22)
  3 dashes of Peychaud's bitters
     Ice
  1 lemon twist

Rinse a chilled rocks glass with the absinthe and pour out the excess. In a mixing glass, combine the rye, Rich Simple Syrup and bitters; fill the glass with ice and stir well. Strain into the prepared rocks glass, pinch the lemon twist over the drink and discard the twist. —*Mike Ryan*

Chancellor

2 ounces single-malt Scotch
½ ounce ruby port
½ ounce dry vermouth
Dash of Peychaud's bitters
Ice

In a mixing glass, combine the Scotch, port, dry vermouth and bitters; fill the glass with ice and stir well. Strain into a chilled coupe. —*Joseph Schwartz*

●●● | 🍸 | Makes: **1**

Joseph Schwartz serves this obscure classic at Little Branch, his New York City speakeasy. Made with Scotch and port, it's a nicely dry variation on the Manhattan.

Monaco Friar

2 ounces Scotch
½ ounce Bénédictine (spiced herbal liqueur)
3 dashes of Angostura bitters
Ice
1 lemon twist, for garnish

In a chilled rocks glass, combine the Scotch, Bénédictine and bitters; fill with ice and stir well. Garnish with the lemon twist. —*Anthony Schmidt*

●●● | ▮ | Makes: **1**

This riff on the classic old-fashioned is best made with a good-quality Scotch. "It's a perfect drink during the colder months," says San Diego bartender Anthony Schmidt.

Brandy

Trends of the decade ● Mixologists give brandy an image makeover, transforming it from an old-fashioned spirit to sip from a snifter into the base for all kinds of inventive cocktails. ● Apple brandies such as Laird's and Calvados make a comeback in classic cocktails like the Jack Rose (p. 124). ● Pisco, the South American brandy, surges in popularity thanks to drinks like the pisco sour (p. 120). ● US stores sell more brandy varieties than ever, including Armagnac and eau-de-vie.

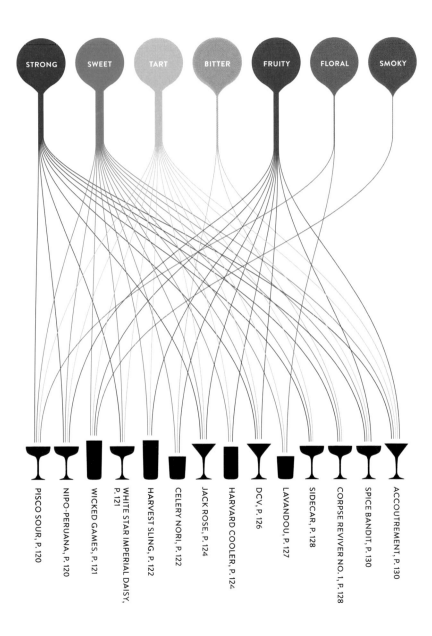

STRONG SWEET TART BITTER FRUITY FLORAL SMOKY

PISCO SOUR, P. 120

NIPO-PERUANA, P. 120

WICKED GAMES, P. 121

WHITE STAR IMPERIAL DAISY, P. 121

HARVEST SLING, P. 122

CELERY NORI, P. 122

JACK ROSE, P. 124

HARVARD COOLER, P. 124

DCV, P. 126

LAVANDOU, P. 127

SIDECAR, P. 128

CORPSE REVIVER NO. 1, P. 128

SPICE BANDIT, P. 130

ACCOUTREMENT, P. 130

Pisco Sour

●●○● | ♈ | Makes: **1**

The national cocktail of Chile and Peru, this drink was invented when a bartender in Lima making a whiskey sour swapped in pisco.

> 2 **ounces pisco**
> ¾ **ounce fresh lime juice**
> ¾ **ounce Simple Syrup (p. 22)**
> 1 **large egg white**
>   **Ice**
> 4 **drops of Angostura bitters, for garnish**

In a cocktail shaker, combine the pisco, lime juice, Simple Syrup and egg white; shake vigorously. Fill the shaker with ice and shake again, then strain into a chilled coupe. Dot the drink with the bitters and draw a straw through the drops. —*Classic*

Nipo-Peruana

●●○● | ♈ | Makes: **1**

"I wanted to revive the Midori Sour and found that pisco worked beautifully in the drink," says L.A. mixologist Lindsay Nader. To cut the cloying sweetness of Midori, a melon liqueur, she adds a good amount of lemon and lime juices.

> 1½ **ounces pisco, preferably Peruvian**
> ½ **ounce melon liqueur**
> ½ **ounce fresh lemon juice**
> ½ **ounce fresh lime juice**
> ½ **ounce orgeat (almond-flavored syrup)**
>   **Ice**
> 3 **honeydew melon balls skewered on a pick, for garnish**

In a cocktail shaker, combine the pisco, melon liqueur, citrus juices and orgeat; fill the shaker with ice and shake well. Strain into a chilled coupe and garnish with the skewered honeydew balls. —*Lindsay Nader*

Wicked Games

1¼ ounces pear eau-de-vie
¾ ounce mezcal
¾ ounce fresh lemon juice
¾ ounce chilled unsweetened pineapple juice
½ ounce Intense Ginger Syrup (below)
    Ice cubes, plus crushed ice (p. 21) for serving

In a cocktail shaker, combine the eau-de-vie, mezcal, juices and Ginger Syrup; fill with ice cubes and shake well. Strain into a chilled, crushed-ice-filled collins glass.

INTENSE GINGER SYRUP

In a saucepan, simmer ½ cup sugar in 4 ounces water, stirring, until dissolved. Add ⅓ cup minced fresh ginger; simmer over low heat for 30 minutes, stirring occasionally. Let cool; pour through a fine strainer into a jar. Refrigerate for up to 2 weeks. Makes about 5 ounces. *—Tommy Klus*

●●● | ▌| Makes: **1**
Time: **5 min** plus simmering and cooling the syrup

Tommy Klus, curator of the Multnomah Whiskey Library in Portland, Oregon, was inspired by a Vietnamese meal to create this pineapple-and-ginger-flavored cocktail. Mezcal gives it a hint of smokiness.

White Star Imperial Daisy

2 ounces Armagnac
½ ounce kümmel (caraway-flavored liqueur)
½ ounce fresh lemon juice
1 teaspoon cane syrup (see Note)
    Ice
1 ounce chilled Champagne

In a cocktail shaker, combine the Armagnac, kümmel, lemon juice and cane syrup; fill the shaker with ice and shake well. Strain into a chilled coupe and stir in the Champagne. *—David Wondrich*

Note Sweet, thick cane syrup is available at Whole Foods and *cocktailkingdom.com*.

 ●● | ⅂ | Makes: **1**

"A daisy," cocktail historian David Wondrich explains, "is a sour sweetened with liqueur." Here he uses kümmel, a liqueur known as "putting mixture" in Scottish golf circles: Many golfers take shots of it to steady nerves before teeing off.

Harvest Sling

●●● | **▌** | Makes: **1**

This Singapore Sling revamp is from John Deragon, a Manhattan-based mixologist. He uses Laird's "bottled-in-bond" apple brandy. That means it's 100 proof, produced by one distiller and stored in a bonded warehouse under US government supervision to guarantee its authenticity.

1½ ounces apple brandy, preferably bonded
¾ ounce sweet vermouth
¾ ounce fresh lemon juice
½ ounce Bénédictine (spiced herbal liqueur)
½ ounce Heering cherry liqueur
   Ice cubes, plus crushed ice (p. 21; optional)
1½ ounces chilled ginger beer
 2 brandied cherries and ½ orange wheel skewered on a pick, for garnish

In a cocktail shaker, combine all the ingredients except the ice, ginger beer and garnishes; fill with ice cubes and shake well. Strain into a chilled, crushed-ice-filled collins glass, stir in the ginger beer and garnish. —*John Deragon*

Celery Nori

●●● | **■** | Makes: **1**

Time: **5 min**

plus steeping

Don Lee created this savory cocktail for Momofuku Ssäm Bar in New York City. He dips nori (the dried seaweed used in sushi) briefly in apple brandy, infusing it with umami.

One 3-inch piece of celery rib, finely chopped
¼ ounce Simple Syrup (p. 22)
 2 ounces Nori Apple Brandy (below)
 2 dashes of celery bitters
   Ice
 1 lemon twist, for garnish

In a mixing glass, lightly muddle the celery with the Simple Syrup. Let steep for 30 minutes, then add the Nori Apple Brandy and the bitters; fill with ice and stir well. Fine-strain (p. 21) into a chilled, ice-filled rocks glass and garnish with the lemon twist.

NORI APPLE BRANDY

In a large bowl, cover 6⅓ sheets (8-by-8-inches) of nori with one 750-ml bottle bonded apple brandy. Let infuse for 90 seconds (really) and strain into a container. Keep for up to 1 month. Makes about 24 ounces. —*Don Lee*

HARVEST SLING

Jack Rose

●●●● | ▼ | Makes: **1**

Time: **5 min** plus
simmering and cooling
the grenadine

"We don't use com-
mercial grenadine,"
says Joseph Schwartz,
co-owner of Little
Branch in Manhattan.
Instead, he sweetens
this classic drink
with his own richly
flavored grenadine.

2   ounces applejack (American apple brandy)
¾   ounce fresh lemon juice
¾   ounce Little Branch Grenadine (below)
    Ice
1   thin Granny Smith apple wedge, for garnish

In a cocktail shaker, combine the applejack, lemon
juice and grenadine; fill the shaker with ice and
shake well. Strain into a chilled martini glass and
garnish with the apple wedge.

LITTLE BRANCH GRENADINE

In a medium saucepan, simmer 1 quart pomegranate
juice over moderate heat until reduced by half. Add
1½ cups sugar and stir until dissolved. Let cool, transfer
to an airtight container and refrigerate for up to
3 weeks. Makes about 16 ounces. —*Joseph Schwartz*

Harvard Cooler

●●● | ▮ | Makes: **1**

According to Hidetsugu
Ueno of Bar High Five
in Tokyo, this somewhat
obscure classic is a
fixture at Japanese bars.
Some people omit
the club soda and call
it a Moonlight.

1½   ounces Calvados
⅓   ounce fresh lemon juice
1   teaspoon Simple Syrup (p. 22)
    Ice
1½   ounces chilled club soda

In a cocktail shaker, combine the Calvados, lemon
juice and Simple Syrup; fill the shaker with ice
and shake well. Strain into a chilled, ice-filled highball
glass, then stir in the club soda. —*Hidetsugu Ueno*

DCV

●●●● | Y | Makes: **1**

This cocktail is from chef Linton Hopkins of Atlanta's Restaurant Eugene. He named the Calvados-based twist on a sidecar (p. 128) after the Citroën 2CV, informally called a Deux Chevaux ("two horsepower"). The midcentury economy auto was known for enduring power that belied its simple, utilitarian design.

1 **tablespoon sugar**
1 **teaspoon cinnamon**
1 **lime wedge**
1½ **ounces Calvados**
1 **ounce Cointreau**
1 **ounce fresh lime juice**
½ **ounce fresh lemon juice**
½ **ounce Simple Syrup (p. 22)**
¼ **ounce St. Elizabeth allspice dram (rum-based allspice liqueur)**
   Ice
1 **apple slice, for garnish**

On a small plate, mix the sugar and cinnamon. Moisten the outer rim of a chilled martini glass with the lime wedge and coat lightly with the cinnamon sugar. In a cocktail shaker, combine the Calvados, Cointreau, citrus juices, Simple Syrup and allspice dram; fill the shaker with ice and shake well. Strain into the prepared glass and garnish with the apple slice. —*Linton Hopkins*

Lavandou

- 1²/₃ ounces Cognac
- ²/₃ ounce fresh lemon juice
- ²/₃ ounce Lavender-Honey Syrup (below)
  Ice
- 1 fresh lavender sprig, for garnish (optional)

In a chilled rocks glass, combine the Cognac, lemon juice and Lavender-Honey Syrup. Fill the glass with ice, stir well and garnish with the lavender sprig.

LAVENDER-HONEY SYRUP

Put 2 teaspoons dried lavender on top of an inverted cocktail shaker. Add ½ ounce Angostura bitters to a small, clean spray bottle (available at drugstores). Spray the bitters over the lavender 6 times, simultaneously flaming the misted bitters with a lit match. Add the lavender to 4 ounces very hot water and let steep for 15 minutes; strain into a small bowl and stir in 4 ounces honey. Refrigerate the syrup for up to 3 weeks. Makes about 8 ounces. *—Romée de Goriainoff*

●● | ▪ | Makes: 1
Time: **10 min** plus
steeping the syrup

Russian-French mixologist Romée de Goriainoff, a partner in the Experimental Cocktail Club (with locations in New York City, Paris and London), has a penchant for lavender: His family creates fragrances from their massive lavender field in France. Here, de Goriainoff makes a lavender-scented honey to mix into a Cognac cocktail.

Sidecar

 | ♀ | Makes: **1**

While many bartenders consider the sugar rim essential to the classic sidecar, Jonny Raglin of San Francisco's Comstock Saloon asks people their preference. "If no rim, then I simply garnish the drink with a twist."

1¾ ounces VSOP Cognac
¾ ounce orange curaçao
¾ ounce fresh lemon juice
¼ ounce Simple Syrup (p. 22)
   Dash of orange bitters
   Ice
1 orange twist, preferably spiral-cut (p. 20), for garnish

In a cocktail shaker, combine the Cognac, curaçao, lemon juice, Simple Syrup and bitters; fill the shaker with ice and shake well. Strain into a chilled coupe and garnish with the orange twist. —*Jonny Raglin*

Corpse Reviver No. 1

●●○ | ♀ | Makes: **1**

This upgrade of the classic morning eye-opener is from Jackson Cannon of Boston's Eastern Standard, The Hawthorne and Island Creek Oyster Bar. The instructions for the original in Harry Craddock's 1930 *Savoy Cocktail Book* direct that the drink be "taken before 11 a.m., or whenever steam and energy are needed."

1 ounce Armagnac
1 ounce Calvados
1 ounce Carpano Antica Formula or other sweet vermouth
   Ice
1 maraschino cherry, for garnish

In a mixing glass, combine the Armagnac, Calvados and vermouth; fill the glass with ice and stir well. Strain into a chilled coupe and garnish with the cherry. —*Jackson Cannon*

Spice Bandit

●●●● | ⏱ | Makes: **1**

Atlanta mixologist Greg Best flavors this cocktail with allspice dram, a rum-based allspice liqueur originally from Jamaica that's also inflected with cinnamon, nutmeg and black pepper.

1½ ounces Cognac
½ ounce Cointreau or other triple sec
½ ounce fresh lime juice
1 teaspoon St. Elizabeth allspice dram
  Ice
1 ounce chilled peach lambic
1 lemon twist, flamed (p. 20), for garnish

In a cocktail shaker, combine the Cognac, Cointreau, lime juice and allspice dram; fill the shaker with ice and shake well. Strain into a chilled coupe, stir in the lambic and garnish with the flamed twist. —*Greg Best*

Accoutrement

●●●● | ⏱ | Makes: **1**

Calvados, a brandy distilled from cider instead of wine, is the base for this spiced cocktail from Chris Hannah of Arnaud's French 75 Bar in New Orleans. Calvados had its golden age in the late 1800s when a phylloxera outbreak devastated the vineyards of Europe; today, mixologists use it in a wide variety of drinks.

2 ounces Calvados
¾ ounce Strega (saffron-infused liqueur)
¾ ounce fresh lemon juice
½ ounce Créole Shrubb (rhum agricole–based orange liqueur) or Grand Marnier
2 dashes of Peychaud's bitters
  Ice
3 brandied cherries, for garnish

In a cocktail shaker, combine the Calvados, Strega, lemon juice, Créole Shrubb and bitters; fill the shaker with ice and shake well. Strain into a chilled martini glass and garnish with the cherries. —*Chris Hannah*

SPICE BANDIT

Nightcaps

Trends of the decade ● Digestifs like limoncello, amaro and grappa, once staples at Italian restaurants, begin to appear in creative cocktails at cutting-edge bars. ● After-dinner drinks with a bitter edge (from dark chocolate, coffee, tea or aged spirits) are in; cloying cocktails (grasshoppers, chocolate martinis, "pie-tinis") are out. ● Flips and other rich egg drinks make a comeback as the concern over raw eggs diminishes. ● Higher-quality liqueurs like crème de cacao inspire better postprandial drinks.

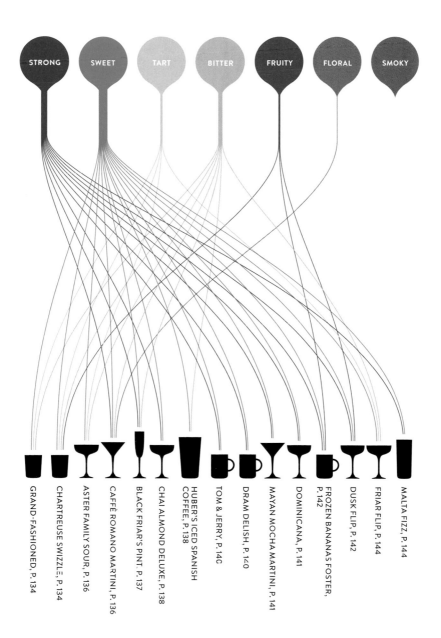

STRONG · SWEET · TART · BITTER · FRUITY · FLORAL · SMOKY

GRAND-FASHIONED, P. 134

CHARTREUSE SWIZZLE, P. 134

ASTER FAMILY SOUR, P. 136

CAFFÈ ROMANO MARTINI, P. 136

BLACK FRIAR'S PINT, P. 137

CHAI ALMOND DELUXE, P. 138

HUBER'S ICED SPANISH COFFEE, P. 138

TOM & JERRY, P. 140

DRAM DELISH, P. 140

MAYAN MOCHA MARTINI, P. 141

DOMINICANA, P. 141

FROZEN BANANAS FOSTER, P. 142

DUSK FLIP, P. 142

FRIAR FLIP, P. 144

MALTA FIZZ, P. 144

Grand-Fashioned

●●● | ▪ | Makes: **1**

This rich, luscious spin on the old-fashioned won first prize in the 1999 New York Film Festival's Independent Cocktail Festival. Some 500 drinks were made for the US premiere of Pedro Almodóvar's *All About My Mother.*

½ blood orange, cut into quarters
½ ounce fresh lime juice
3 dashes of Angostura bitters
1 teaspoon superfine sugar
2 ounces Grand Marnier
   Ice

In a cocktail shaker, muddle the blood orange with the lime juice, bitters and sugar. Add the Grand Marnier and enough ice to fill a rocks glass and shake well. Pour—don't strain—into a chilled rocks glass.
—*Employees Only, New York City*

Chartreuse Swizzle

●●●● | ▪ | Makes: **1**

Green Chartreuse forms the base of this drink from Marcovaldo Dionysos of Smuggler's Cove in San Francisco. While the sweeter yellow Chartreuse is the go-to choice in classic cocktails, spicy, herbal green Chartreuse is a cult favorite among innovative bartenders today.

1¼ ounces green Chartreuse
1 ounce chilled unsweetened pineapple juice
½ ounce Velvet Falernum (clove-spiced liqueur)
½ ounce fresh lime juice
   Ice cubes, plus crushed ice (p. 21) for serving
1 mint sprig and freshly grated nutmeg, for garnish

In a cocktail shaker, combine the Chartreuse, pineapple juice, Velvet Falernum and lime juice; fill the shaker with ice cubes and shake well. Strain into a chilled, crushed-ice-filled rocks glass and garnish with the mint sprig and nutmeg.
—*Marcovaldo Dionysos*

●STRONG ●SWEET ●TART ●BITTER ●FRUITY ●FLORAL ●SMOKY

Aster Family Sour

●●○ | �-down-Y | Makes: **1**

The predominant ingredient in Cynar is artichoke, a member of the aster family. While the herbal liqueur is traditionally served as an aperitif, Zane Harris of Evelyn's in New York City uses it in this delicious bittersweet sour.

1½ ounces Cynar
 1 ounce fresh lemon juice
 ½ ounce orgeat (almond-flavored syrup)
 1 large egg white
   Ice
 2 dashes of Angostura bitters, for garnish

In a cocktail shaker, combine the Cynar, lemon juice, orgeat and egg white and shake vigorously; fill the shaker with ice and shake again. Strain into a chilled coupe, add the bitters and swirl decoratively.
—*Zane Harris*

Caffè Romano Martini

●●●○ | � | Makes: **1**

Mixology consultant Philip Duff created this boozy version of an *espresso romano* (espresso served with a lemon twist). While lemon isn't traditionally served with espresso in Italy, cafés in other parts of the world use the oil in lemon peel to offset the bitterness of the coffee.

 2 ounces chilled brewed espresso
1½ ounces vodka
 ½ ounce coffee liqueur
 ½ ounce elderflower syrup
 ¼ ounce Rich Simple Syrup (p. 22)
   Ice
 3 coffee beans and 1 lemon verbena leaf (optional), smacked (p. 21), for garnish

In a cocktail shaker, combine the espresso, vodka, coffee liqueur, elderflower syrup and Rich Simple Syrup; fill the shaker with ice and shake very well. Strain into a chilled martini glass and garnish with the coffee beans and lemon verbena leaf. —*Philip Duff*

Black Friar's Pint

2 ounces gin
1 ounce Cardamom-Cinnamon Guinness
  (below)
¾ ounce Lustau East India Solera sherry
  Dash of Angostura bitters
1 teaspoon agave nectar
1 large egg white
  Ice
  Pinch of ground cinnamon, for garnish

In a cocktail shaker, combine the gin, Cardamom-
Cinnamon Guinness, sherry, bitters, agave nectar
and egg white and shake vigorously; fill the shaker
with ice and shake again. Strain into a chilled flute
and garnish with the cinnamon.

CARDAMOM-CINNAMON GUINNESS

In a small saucepan, lightly muddle 2 cardamom
pods with 1 cinnamon stick. Add 8 ounces Guinness
stout and bring to a boil. Lower the heat and simmer
for 1 minute. Let cool, then strain the spiced Guinness
into a jar, cover and refrigerate for up to 3 weeks.
Makes about 8 ounces. — *Jacques Bezuidenhout*

 | ! | Makes: **1**

Before Jacques
Bezuidenhout began
mixing innovative cock-
tails for the Kimpton
Hotels & Restaurants'
bars throughout the
US, he poured pints of
Guinness at a pub.
"When I shake this drink
with an egg white, it
froths and slowly set-
tles like a mini pint of
Guinness," he says.

Chai Almond Deluxe

●● | ⊤ | Makes: **1**

Time: **5 min**

plus infusing

Drinks consultant
Chad Solomon created
the Chai Almond
Deluxe to demonstrate
Cognac's versatility.
The drink is his twist on
a zoom, a category of
cocktails that incorpo-
rate cream and honey.

   2 ounces Chai-Infused Cognac (below)
1½ ounces vanilla almond milk
  ¼ ounce Honey Syrup (p. 22)
  ½ teaspoon pure vanilla extract
   1 large egg white
      Ice

In a cocktail shaker, combine the infused Cognac,
almond milk, Honey Syrup, vanilla and egg white
and shake vigorously; fill with ice and shake again.
Strain into a chilled coupe.

CHAI-INFUSED COGNAC
In a jar, combine 8 ounces Cognac with 2 chai tea
bags. Let stand for 2 hours. Discard the tea; refrigerate
up to 1 week. Makes 8 ounces. —*Chad Solomon*

Huber's Iced Spanish Coffee

●● | ❚ | Makes: **1**

Huber's, Portland's old-
est restaurant, opened
as a saloon in 1879.
Over the years, Spanish
coffee (made table-
side with flames and
fanfare) became its sig-
nature drink. It's so
popular that Huber's
is now the largest inde-
pendent restaurant
user of Kahlúa in the US.

  ¾ ounce overproof rum
  ¼ ounce triple sec
1½ ounces coffee liqueur, preferably Kahlúa
      Ice
   4 ounces chilled strong coffee
  ¼ cup unsweetened whipped cream
      Freshly grated nutmeg, for garnish

In a saucepan, combine the rum and triple sec and
ignite with a long match. Carefully add the coffee
liqueur; pour the flaming mixture into a chilled, ice-filled
pint glass. Stir in the coffee, top with the whipped
cream and garnish with nutmeg. —*Huber's, Portland, OR*

HUBER'S ICED
SPANISH COFFEE

Tom & Jerry

●● | ▶ | Makes: **4**

Time: **15 min**

John Gertsen started serving this classic hot Christmas cocktail at Boston's No. 9 Park in 2004. He has since amassed a collection of antique Tom & Jerry sets (bowls with matching cups), mostly from the Midwest, where the tradition of the drink lives on.

8	ounces Tom & Jerry Batter (below)
4	ounces Cognac
4	ounces aged rum
8	ounces hot whole milk
	Freshly grated nutmeg, for garnish

Pour the Tom & Jerry Batter into a large heatproof measuring cup. Gently fold in the Cognac and rum, then gently stir in the hot milk. Pour the drink into 4 small warmed mugs or heatproof glasses. Garnish with nutmeg.

TOM & JERRY BATTER

In a medium bowl, beat 3 large egg whites with ⅛ teaspoon cream of tartar until soft peaks form. In another bowl, beat 3 egg yolks with ½ ounce aged rum; gradually beat in 1 cup superfine sugar, ⅛ teaspoon ground cinnamon, ⅛ teaspoon ground mace, ⅛ teaspoon ground allspice and a small pinch of ground cloves. Gently fold in the beaten egg whites. The batter can be refrigerated overnight. Makes about 20 ounces. *—John Gertsen*

Dram Delish

●● | ▶ | Makes: **1**

For this hot spiked drink, Jeff Grdinich, bar manager at The Rose in Jackson Hole, Wyoming, makes super-indulgent hot cocoa with cream rather than milk.

1½	ounces aged rhum agricole
¾	ounce maraschino liqueur
½	ounce St. Elizabeth allspice dram (allspice liqueur)
4	ounces hot chocolate
	Dollop of lightly sweetened whipped cream, for garnish
1	star anise pod, for garnish (optional)

In a warmed mug or heatproof glass, mix the rhum with both liqueurs, then stir in the hot chocolate. Garnish with the whipped cream and star anise. *—Jeff Grdinich*

Mayan Mocha Martini

1½ ounces blanco tequila
¾ ounce half-and-half
½ ounce coffee liqueur
½ ounce dark crème de cacao
   Ice
   Pinch each of cinnamon and cayenne pepper,
   for garnish

In a cocktail shaker, combine the tequila, half-and-half, coffee liqueur and crème de cacao and shake vigorously; fill the shaker with ice and shake again. Strain into a chilled martini glass and garnish with the cinnamon and cayenne. —James Lee

●● | ▼ | Makes: 1

Austin bartender James Lee combines tequila, Mexican coffee liqueur and crème de cacao to evoke the flavors of two Mexican specialties: Ibarra chocolate (used to make Mexican hot chocolate) and *café de olla*, a traditional spiced coffee.

Dominicana

1 ounce heavy cream
¼ ounce Simple Syrup (p. 22)
   Ice
1½ ounces añejo rum
1½ ounces coffee liqueur

In a cocktail shaker, combine the cream, Simple Syrup and 1 ice cube. Shake vigorously to aerate the cream and melt the ice. In a mixing glass, combine the rum and liqueur; fill the glass with ice and stir well. Strain into a chilled coupe and spoon the whipped cream on top. —Sasha Petraske

●● | ▼ | Makes: 1

Sasha Petraske first made this rum-based White Russian variation in 2000 at Milk & Honey, his influential New York City speakeasy. Petraske stirs in Caffé Lolita coffee liqueur, which has a rich, chocolate-inflected flavor.

Frozen Bananas Foster

●●● | ◗ | Makes: **6**

When master mixologist Adam Seger was five years old, his parents bought him a blender. Inspired by the Bananas Foster at Brennan's Restaurant in New Orleans, Seger began perfecting banana smoothies. "Who knew that this obsession would lead to a career?" he says.

10 ounces bourbon

4 bananas

4 ounces fresh orange juice

1 cup caramel sauce

1 pint vanilla ice cream

3 cups ice

   Freshly grated nutmeg and 6 cinnamon sticks, for garnish

In a blender, combine the bourbon, bananas, orange juice, caramel sauce, ice cream and ice and blend until smooth. Pour into chilled mugs. Garnish each drink with grated nutmeg and a cinnamon stick.
—*Adam Seger*

Dusk Flip

●●● | ▽ | Makes: **1**

"This is the drink I would choose instead of dessert after a big meal," says L.A. mixologist John Coltharp. Fruity, spicy Redbreast Irish whiskey is excellent with the blackberries.

3 blackberries, plus 1 blackberry skewered on a pick for garnish

2 ounces Irish whiskey

1 large egg

½ ounce heavy cream

½ ounce Simple Syrup (p. 22)

   Ice

   Small pinch of freshly grated nutmeg, for garnish

In a cocktail shaker, muddle the 3 blackberries. Add the whiskey, egg, cream and Simple Syrup and shake vigorously. Fill the shaker with ice and shake again. Fine-strain (p. 21) into a chilled coupe and garnish with the skewered berry and nutmeg. —*John Coltharp*

Friar Flip

●●● | ♈ | Makes: **1**

"So many guests are intrigued by eggs in cocktails, I wanted to make a flip [a spiced, nog-like drink]," says Melissa Hayes, a bartender at Leon's Full Service in Decatur, Georgia. She spices the drink with chocolaty mole bitters and yellow Chartreuse, a honeyed herbal liqueur made by monks since the 1700s.

1 ounce yellow Chartreuse
½ ounce Bonal Gentiane-Quina (fortified, slightly bitter aperitif wine)
½ ounce Simple Syrup (p. 22)
½ ounce fresh lemon juice
4 dashes of Bittermens Xocolatl Mole bitters
Pinch of salt
1 large egg
Ice
Pinch of freshly grated nutmeg, for garnish

In a cocktail shaker, combine all of the ingredients except ice and the garnish and shake vigorously; fill the shaker with ice and shake again. Strain the drink into a chilled coupe and garnish with the freshly grated nutmeg. —*Melissa Hayes*

Malta Fizz

●● | ▮ | Makes: **1**

Mixologist Jose "Juice" Miranda based the Malta Fizz on a traditional Latin American drink his mother made for him as a child: egg yolk, sugar, condensed milk and malta, a nonalcoholic carbonated malt beverage (available at Latin markets).

2 ounces amber rum
2 ounces malta
1 ounce Simple Syrup (p. 22)
¾ ounce fresh lime juice
1 large egg yolk
Ice
1 cinnamon stick (optional) and pinch of ground cinnamon, for garnish

In a cocktail shaker, combine the rum, malta, Simple Syrup, lime juice and egg yolk; shake vigorously. Fill the shaker with ice and shake again. Strain into a chilled, ice-filled collins glass and garnish with the cinnamon. —*Jose Miranda*

Big-Batch Drinks

Trends of the decade ● Cocktail historian David Wondrich's seminal 2010 book *Punch* inspires the return of punch bowls to bars. ● New ice shapes, including large blocks, pave the way for striking punch and pitcher-drink presentations. ● In: unadorned punches served in vintage bowls and cups (increasingly available on eBay and other online sources). Out: tricked-out pitcher drinks like sangria jam-packed with fruit. ● Cocktails on tap push the boundaries of what is considered a big-batch drink.

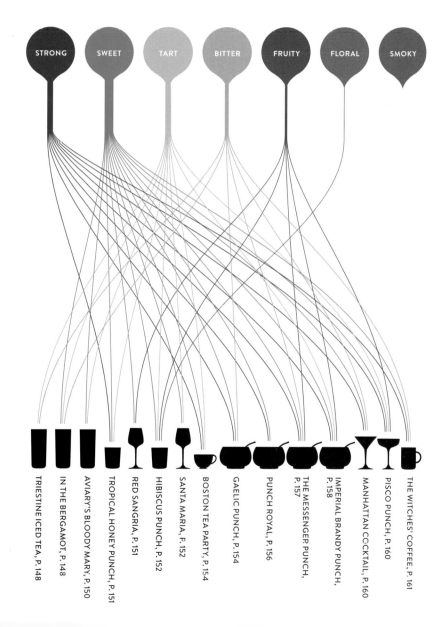

STRONG SWEET TART BITTER FRUITY FLORAL SMOKY

TRIESTINE ICED TEA, P. 148

IN THE BERGAMOT, P. 148

AVIARY'S BLOODY MARY, P. 150

TROPICAL HONEY PUNCH, P. 151

RED SANGRIA, P. 151

HIBISCUS PUNCH, P. 152

SANTA MARIA, P. 152

BOSTON TEA PARTY, P. 154

GAELIC PUNCH, P. 154

PUNCH ROYAL, P. 156

THE MESSENGER PUNCH, P. 157

THE MESSENGER PUNCH, P. 158

IMPERIAL BRANDY PUNCH, P. 158

MANHATTAN COCKTAIL, P. 160

PISCO PUNCH, P. 160

THE WITCHES' COFFEE, P. 161

Triestine Iced Tea

●● | ▮ | Makes: **8**

Time: **5 min** plus chilling

Limoncello and club soda temper Cynar's intense bitterness and give it the color of iced tea in this drink from Boulder, Colorado's Frasca Food and Wine.

16 ounces Cynar (bitter artichoke aperitif)
8 ounces limoncello
   Ice
20 ounces chilled club soda
8 lemon wedges, for garnish

In a pitcher, combine the Cynar and limoncello and refrigerate until chilled, about 2 hours. Stir, then pour into 8 chilled, ice-filled collins glasses. Stir 2½ ounces of club soda into each drink and garnish with the lemon wedges. —*Frasca Food and Wine, Boulder, CO*

In the Bergamot

●●● | ▮ | Makes: **8**

Time: **30 min**

plus chilling

Earl Grey tea–infused vermouth adds fragrant citrus flavor to this aperitif-style pitcher drink. According to Ira Koplowitz and Nicholas Kosevich, founders of Bittercube artisanal bitters, the herbal ingredients here help awaken the palate and soothe the stomach.

3 Earl Grey tea bags
8 ounces Cocchi Vermouth di Torino or other sweet vermouth
8 ounces Aperol
8 ounces bourbon
½ ounce orange bitters
   Ice
16 ounces chilled club soda
8 spiral-cut orange twists (p. 20), for garnish

In a bowl, cover the tea bags with the vermouth; let steep for 20 minutes, then strain into a pitcher. Stir in the Aperol, bourbon and bitters and refrigerate until chilled, about 2 hours. Stir, then pour into 8 chilled, ice-filled collins glasses. Stir 2 ounces of club soda into each drink and garnish with the orange twists. —*Ira Koplowitz and Nicholas Kosevich*

Aviary's Bloody Mary

●● | ❙ | Makes: **2**

Time: **30 min**

plus freezing

This deconstructed Bloody Mary can be made year-round with bottled tomato juice, but Craig Schoettler, who made this drink at The Aviary in Chicago, uses ripe tomatoes in season. He adds colorful ice cubes that flavor the drink as they slowly melt: Green celery ice cubes, black Worcestershire sauce ones and red cubes that get their color and flavor from chiles. This way, he says, "The palate doesn't get bored. The drink is 'new' with every sip."

4   each of Celery, Fresno Chile and Worcestershire Ice Cubes (below)
12   ounces chilled tomato juice
5½   ounces vodka
¾   ounce Simple Syrup (p. 22)
½   teaspoon salt
    Freshly cracked black pepper, celery ribs and parsley sprigs, for garnish (optional)

Fill 2 chilled collins glasses with 2 cubes each of the Celery, Fresno Chile and Worcestershire Ice Cubes. In a pitcher, combine the tomato juice, vodka, Simple Syrup and salt and stir well. Pour the Bloody Mary mixture over the ice cubes and garnish the drinks with cracked black pepper, celery ribs and parsley.

CELERY ICE CUBES
Using a juice extractor, juice 2 blanched celery ribs. Add ½ teaspoon each of salt and sugar to the juice and stir well. Makes 4 cubes in a standard ice tray.

FRESNO CHILE ICE CUBES
Using a juice extractor, juice 2 stemmed Fresno or 6 Thai chiles. Add 4 ounces water to the juice and stir well. Makes 4 cubes in a standard ice tray.

WORCESTERSHIRE ICE CUBES
Combine 2 ounces Worcestershire sauce with 3 ounces water. Makes 4 cubes in a standard ice tray.

—*Craig Schoettler*

Tropical Honey Punch

8   ounces London dry gin
6   ounces fresh lemon juice
4   ounces aged rum, preferably Jamaican
4   ounces Velvet Falernum (clove-spiced liqueur)
4   ounces Honey Syrup (p. 22)
8   dashes of Angostura bitters
1   big block of ice, plus 8 large ice cubes for serving (p. 21)
8   ounces chilled sparkling water
8   lemon wheels, 8 pineapple spears and cinnamon, for garnish

In a punch bowl, combine all of the ingredients except the ice, sparkling water and garnishes and refrigerate until chilled, about 2 hours. Stir well, then add the big block of ice and the sparkling water. Place 1 large ice cube into each of 8 chilled rocks glasses and ladle the punch over the ice. Garnish each drink with 1 lemon wheel, 1 pineapple spear and a pinch of cinnamon. —*Erick Castro*

 | ▮ | Makes: **8**

Time: **20 min**

plus chilling

"Many people only think of rum in tiki drinks," says Erick Castro of Polite Provisions in San Diego, "but gin played a large role in the history of tropical cocktails." The British Royal Navy sailed with gin on voyages throughout the Caribbean and mixed it with local ingredients.

Red Sangria

One 750-ml bottle of fruity red wine, such as Merlot
4   ounces brandy
3   ounces Simple Syrup (p. 22)
1   cup mixed chunks of seeded orange, lemon and lime
Ice

In a pitcher, combine the wine, brandy, Simple Syrup and fruit and refrigerate until chilled, 4 to 8 hours. Serve the sangria in chilled, ice-filled wineglasses. —*Bridget Albert*

 | ♀ | Makes: **6**

Time: **10 min**

plus chilling

"My family always expects me to make cocktails," says master mixologist Bridget Albert. "Making a batch of sangria means I don't have to wait on everyone all night, so I can enjoy a glass or two!"

Hibiscus Punch

●●●● | ▪ | Makes: **12**

Time: **30 min**

plus chilling

Star mixologist Kathy Casey loves punches for large parties because they can be made ahead of time. Her Hibiscus Punch has a tart, tropical flavor and a gorgeous magenta color.

1 cup dried hibiscus flowers or loose hibiscus tea
1½ cups honey
32 ounces vodka
8 ounces fresh lime juice
4 ounces chilled unsweetened pineapple juice
1 teaspoon Angostura bitters
Ice
Lime wheels, for garnish

In a large heatproof bowl, cover the hibiscus flowers with 48 ounces boiling water; let steep for 10 minutes. Strain into a large heatproof jar, stir in the honey and let cool; refrigerate the flowers. Stir the vodka into the hibiscus liquid; refrigerate until chilled, about 2 hours. Stir in the lime juice, pineapple juice and bitters. Pour into chilled, ice-filled double rocks glasses and garnish with the hibiscus flowers and lime wheels. —*Kathy Casey*

Santa Maria

●● | ⍨ | Makes: **8**

Time: **15 min**

plus chilling

Duggan McDonnell of Cantina in San Francisco describes this crowd-pleasing punch as bright, aromatic and refreshing.

12 ounces blanco tequila
8 ounces fresh lemon juice
6 ounces white port
2 ounces Velvet Falernum (clove-spiced liqueur)
2 ounces agave nectar mixed with 2 ounces water
Ice
6 ounces chilled ginger beer
8 orange wheels, for garnish

In a large resealable container, combine the tequila, lemon juice, port, Velvet Falernum and agave syrup; refrigerate until chilled, about 1 hour. Cover tightly and shake, then pour into an ice-filled pitcher. Strain into 8 chilled, ice-filled wineglasses, stir in the ginger beer and garnish with the orange wheels. —*Duggan McDonnell*

HIBISCUS PUNCH

Boston Tea Party

●●● | ● | Makes: **6**

Time: **10 min**

plus chilling

Jacques Bezuidenhout of Kimpton Hotels & Restaurants riffs on Ti'Punch, an aperitif popular in the French Caribbean that's traditionally served chilled, without ice.

- 12 ounces chilled brewed chai
- 9 ounces aged rhum agricole
- 1½ ounces Créole Shrubb or Grand Marnier
- 1½ ounces fresh lime juice
- 6 spiral-cut orange twists (p. 20), for garnish

In a pitcher, combine the chai, rhum agricole, Créole Shrubb and lime juice and refrigerate until chilled, about 1 hour. Stir, then strain into chilled tea cups and garnish with the twists.
—*Jacques Bezuidenhout*

Gaelic Punch

●●● | ● | Makes: **14**

Time: **15 min**

plus macerating

According to cocktail historian David Wondrich, whiskey punch was a staple of the Irish from the mid-1700s until the mid-1800s, when it was replaced by stout. For the punch here, Wondrich recommends a young Irish whiskey.

   Strips of zest from 6 lemons
- ¾ cup Demerara or other raw sugar
- 40 ounces boiling water
One 750-ml bottle of Irish whiskey
   Pinch of freshly grated nutmeg and 6 thin lemon slices, each studded with 4 cloves, for garnish

In a heatproof bowl, muddle the lemon zest strips with the sugar and let stand for 1 to 2 hours. Muddle again, add 8 ounces of the boiling water and stir until the sugar dissolves. Strain into a warmed heatproof punch bowl and stir in the whiskey. Add the remaining 32 ounces of boiling water and garnish the punch with the nutmeg and studded lemon slices. —*David Wondrich*

BOSTON TEA PARTY
Cocktail pins by
Watakoma from
Umami Mart.

Punch Royal

●● | 🍶 | Makes: **24**

Time: **15 min** plus
infusing and chilling

"Punch Royal dates back to the end of the 17th century," says David Wondrich, author of *Punch: The Delights and Dangers of the Flowing Bowl.* It combines punch, favored by progressives, and wine, favored by conservatives. "In Punch Royal, the two get along famously."

One 1-liter bottle of Cognac
    Large strips of zest from 2 lemons
1 pound *panela* (Latin American solid sugar) or light brown sugar
1 cinnamon stick
1 teaspoon finely grated fresh ginger
8 ounces fresh lemon juice
One-half 750-ml bottle of chilled dry German Riesling
    Ice, preferably 1 large block (p. 21)
    Freshly grated nutmeg, for garnish

1. In a large container, combine the Cognac and lemon zest strips and let stand at room temperature for 6 to 8 hours. Discard the lemon zest.

2. In a large saucepan, combine the sugar, cinnamon stick and ginger with 16 ounces of water. Cook over low heat, stirring, until the sugar dissolves, about 3 minutes. Strain the brown sugar syrup and let cool.

3. In a large punch bowl, combine the infused Cognac with the lemon juice and three-quarters of the brown sugar syrup; refrigerate until chilled, about 2 hours. Stir in the Riesling and 32 ounces of chilled water; add more brown sugar syrup to taste. Add the ice and garnish with freshly grated nutmeg. —*David Wondrich*

The Messenger Punch

12 ounces fresh lemon juice
 8 ounces pear liqueur
 8 ounces chilled unsweetened pineapple juice
 2 ounces orgeat (almond-flavored syrup)
1½ ounces Don's Spices #2 (*bgreynolds.com*) or
    1½ ounces Vanilla Spice Syrup (below)
16 dashes of Fee Brothers Whiskey Barrel–Aged
    bitters or Angostura bitters
One 750-ml bottle of bonded apple brandy
32 ounces chilled club soda
    Ice, preferably 1 large block (p. 21)

In a punch bowl, combine the lemon juice, pear liqueur, pineapple juice, orgeat, Don's Spices and bitters. Add the apple brandy and refrigerate until chilled, about 2 hours. Stir in the club soda and add the ice.

VANILLA SPICE SYRUP

In a jar, combine 1 split vanilla bean, 5 allspice berries, 1 cup sugar and 8 ounces water. Let stand at room temperature, stirring occasionally, for 24 hours. Strain, cover and refrigerate for up to 2 weeks. Makes about 12 ounces. —*Jason Littrell and Hal Wolin*

●●●● | 🍎 | Makes: **16**
Time: **10 min** plus
steeping and chilling

"This punch is a compilation of my 'desert island' ingredients," says New York City hospitality consultant Jason Littrell. The punch, equally suitable in summer and winter, "is incredibly versatile but deceptively boozy."

Imperial Brandy Punch

●●●● | 🍸 | Makes: **20**

Time: **15 min**

plus chilling

The original version of this punch appeared in the 1882 edition of *Harry Johnson's New and Improved Bartenders' Manual*. Instead of using seltzer, which can dilute the drink, Wayne Collins stirs in Champagne. "It adds a nice sparkle and a delicate wine character to lift the whole mix," says Collins, who runs the U.K. bartender training program Mixxit.

One 1-liter bottle of Cognac
½ liter amber rum
10 ounces fresh lemon juice
6 ounces Raspberry Syrup (below)
5 ounces curaçao or triple sec
Two 750-ml bottles of chilled Champagne
   Ice, preferably 1 large block (p. 21)
5 sliced oranges and 1 cubed pineapple, for garnish

In a punch bowl, combine the Cognac, rum, lemon juice, Raspberry Syrup and curaçao and refrigerate until chilled, about 4 hours. Gently stir in the Champagne. Add the ice and garnish with the orange slices and pineapple cubes.

RASPBERRY SYRUP

In a saucepan, combine 12 ounces raspberry jam with 8 ounces water. Cook over moderate heat, stirring, until the jam is melted, about 5 minutes. Strain into a heatproof jar and let cool completely. Cover and refrigerate for up to 1 month. Makes about 16 ounces. —*Wayne Collins*

IMPERIAL
BRANDY PUNCH

● STRONG ● SWEET ● TART ● BITTER ● FRUITY ● FLORAL ● SMOKY

Manhattan Cocktail

●●○ | ʏ | Makes: **8**

The Manhattan Cocktail served at New York City's Employees Only uses a nearly forgotten 19th-century formula: It has a higher ratio of sweet vermouth to rye than the modern Manhattan.

11 ounces sweet vermouth
11 ounces rye whiskey
2½ ounces Grand Marnier
16 dashes of Angostura bitters
    Ice
8   orange or lemon twists, for garnish

In a pitcher, combine the vermouth, rye, Grand Marnier and bitters; fill two-thirds of the pitcher with ice and stir for 30 seconds to chill. Strain into 8 chilled martini glasses and garnish each with a twist. —*Employees Only, New York City*

Pisco Punch

●●●○ | ʏ | Makes: **12**
Time: **20 min**
plus chilling

"Pisco Punch raises lots of questions," says Erik Adkins of The Slanted Door in San Francisco. "Lemon or lime? Was cocaine the secret ingredient?" There are no definitive answers about this classic punch: It's said that the inventor, saloon owner Duncan Nicol, took the original recipe to his grave.

24 ounces pisco
8   ounces fresh lemon juice (from about 6 lemons)
One 8½-fluid-ounce bottle of pineapple gum syrup (see Note)
2½ cups fresh pineapple chunks
    Ice, preferably 1 large block (p. 21)
    Thin pineapple slices, for garnish

In a punch bowl, combine the pisco, lemon juice, gum syrup and pineapple chunks with 8 ounces of water and refrigerate until chilled, about 2 hours. Add the ice. Serve the punch in chilled coupes and garnish with pineapple slices. —*Erik Adkins*

Note Golden-colored pineapple gum syrup— thickened, pineapple-flavored simple syrup—is available at *smallhandfoods.com*.

The Witches' Coffee

- **4 teaspoons Demerara or other raw sugar**
- **12 ounces hot brewed coffee**
- **6 ounces aged rum, preferably Ron Zacapa 23**
- **3 ounces Strega (saffron-infused liqueur)**
  Averna Cream (below), for garnish

In a heatproof pitcher, stir the sugar into the coffee until dissolved, then stir in the rum and Strega. Pour the coffee into warmed mugs or heatproof glasses and spoon the Averna Cream on top.

AVERNA CREAM

In a chilled bowl, whip 4 ounces chilled heavy cream with 1 ounce Averna amaro and ½ tablespoon sugar until soft peaks form. Use the cream immediately. Makes enough for 4 drinks. —Bryan Dayton

●●● | ● | Makes: **4**

Bryan Dayton, co-owner of Oak at Fourteenth in Boulder, Colorado, totes this hot drink in a thermos to football games and ski trips. "The whipped cream with amaro folded into it is off the hook," he says.

Mocktails

Trends of the decade ● Higher-quality mixers (both commercial and house-made) such as ginger beer and syrups like grenadine and orgeat give rise to tastier virgin cocktails. ● The fresh-juice craze, fueled by powerful blenders and extractors, inspires delicious mocktails. ● Sweeteners ranging from agave nectar to molasses help bartenders prepare better drinks for teetotalers. ● Mixologists add savory ingredients–herbs, spices, teas–to their mocktail arsenal to re-create the thrill and complexity of cocktails.

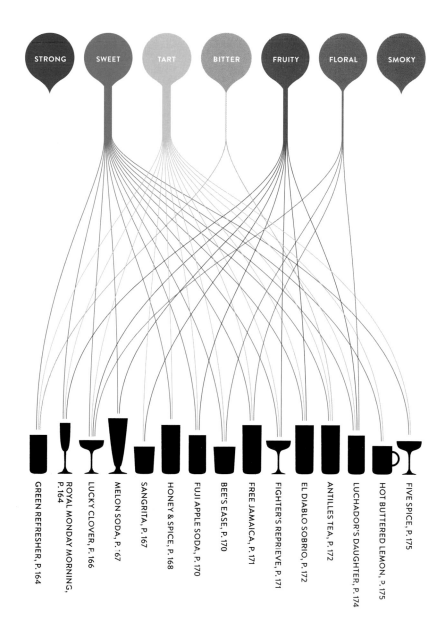

STRONG SWEET TART BITTER FRUITY FLORAL SMOKY

GREEN REFRESHER, P. 164

ROYAL MONDAY MORNING, P. 164

LUCKY CLOVER, P. 166

MELON SODA, P. 167

SANGRITA, P. 167

HONEY & SPICE, P. 168

FUJI APPLE SODA, P. 170

BEE'S EASE, P. 170

FREE JAMAICA, P. 171

FIGHTER'S REPRIEVE, P. 171

EL DIABLO SOBRIO, P. 172

ANTILLES TEA, P. 172

LUCHADOR'S DAUGHTER, P. 174

HOT BUTTERED LEMON, P. 175

FIVE SPICE, P. 175

Green Refresher

●●● | ▌ | Makes: **1**

Green tea and cucumber make this mocktail ultra-cooling. Sebastian Reaburn, head bartender at The Lui Bar in Melbourne, Australia, says to be sure to zest the garnish over the glass; the peel's essential oils give the drink a delightful limy scent.

2   cucumber slices
3   ounces chilled brewed green tea, preferably sencha
1   ounce chilled unfiltered apple juice
¾   ounce Simple Syrup (p. 22)
½   ounce fresh lime juice
    Ice
    Thin strips of lime zest, for garnish

In a chilled highball glass, muddle the cucumber slices, then add the tea, apple juice, Simple Syrup and lime juice. Half-fill the glass with ice and stir well. Add more ice and stir again. Garnish with the lime zest. —*Sebastian Reaburn*

Royal Monday Morning

●●● | ! | Makes: **1**

Based on the Royal Sunday Morning (p. 29), this virgin adaptation by John deBary (assistant editor and recipe tester for *F&W Cocktails 2013*) is best made with a not-too-sweet grapefruit soda.

1   ounce fresh grapefruit juice
1   tablespoon raspberry preserves
    Ice
3   ounces chilled club soda
2   ounces chilled Italian grapefruit soda, such as San Pellegrino Pompelmo

In a cocktail shaker, combine the grapefruit juice and preserves. Fill the shaker with ice and shake well. Strain into a chilled flute or coupe and stir in both sodas. —*John deBary*

Lucky Clover

●●❑●| ⏱ | Makes: **1**

Time: **15 min** plus

steeping and cooling

When Julie Reiner
opened Clover Club in
Brooklyn, New York,
she made sure to
have a roster of good
mocktails like the
Lucky Clover available.
"I created this nonalco-
holic version of our
house cocktail for the
expectant mothers
in the neighborhood,"
she says.

2 **ounces Raspberry Syrup (below)**
2 **ounces fresh lemon juice**
2 **dashes of orange flower water**
1 **medium egg white**
   Ice
3 **raspberries skewered on a pick, for garnish**

In a cocktail shaker, combine the Raspberry Syrup,
lemon juice, orange flower water and egg white
and shake vigorously. Fill the shaker with ice
and shake again. Strain into a chilled coupe and
garnish with the skewered raspberries.

RASPBERRY SYRUP

In a saucepan, combine 6 ounces (about ½ pint)
raspberries with 4 ounces water and ¾ cup
superfine sugar. Cook over low heat for 15 minutes,
smashing the raspberries. Remove from the heat
and let stand for 30 minutes. Strain the raspberry
syrup into a jar, cover and refrigerate for up
to 4 days. Makes about 8 ounces. —*Julie Reiner*

Melon Soda

1½ cups Demerara or other raw sugar

  2 tablespoons chopped dill fronds

  2 tablespoons chopped cilantro

20 ounces fresh cantaloupe juice (from 1 medium cantaloupe, juiced and strained)

1. In a saucepan, stir the sugar with 6 ounces of water over low heat until dissolved. Add the herbs; simmer for 10 minutes. Take off the heat; let steep for 20 minutes.

2. Strain the herb-infused syrup into a bowl and stir in the cantaloupe juice. Pour into a soda siphon (see Note) and refrigerate until chilled, about 1 hour. Seal the canister, shake hard and charge according to the manufacturer's directions with 1 or 2 CO_2 chargers. Dispense the soda into 8 chilled pilsner glasses. —Daniel Shoemaker

Note Soda siphons and CO_2 chargers are available at kitchenware shops and amazon.com.

●● | ❗ | Makes: **8**
Time: **15 min** plus
steeping and chilling

"I wanted a drink that was juicy and loaded with succulence," says Daniel Shoemaker of Teardrop Cocktail Lounge in Portland, Oregon. He came up with this homemade cantaloupe soda, which can also be mixed into cocktails.

Sangrita

15 ounces chilled tomato juice

  7 ounces fresh orange juice

  3 ounces fresh grapefruit juice

  2 ounces hot sauce

1¼ ounces fresh lime juice

 ½ jalapeño (with seeds for a spicier drink)

1½ teaspoons freshly ground pepper

  1 teaspoon salt

In a pitcher, combine all of the ingredients and stir until the salt is dissolved. Let stand for 15 minutes (30 minutes for a spicier drink). Discard the jalapeño and refrigerate until chilled, 2 hours. Stir well and pour into 4 chilled rocks glasses. —Jacques Bezuidenhout

●● | ▪ | Makes: **4**
Time: **10 min** plus
standing and chilling

This spicy tomato drink is typically served as a chaser for tequila, but the version by Jacques Bezuidenhout of Kimpton Hotels & Restaurants is delicious on its own.

Honey & Spice

 | **I** | Makes: **1**

Time: **10 min**

plus steeping

"I loved Orange Julius when I was a kid," says Jennifer Colliau, founder of Small Hand Foods artisanal syrups. "I tried to get one every time my mom took me to the mall." She creates Creamsicle-like flavors in this drink with grapefruit, honey and allspice.

1½ ounces fresh grapefruit juice
1 ounce fresh lime juice
½ ounce Honey Syrup (p. 22)
½ ounce Allspice Syrup (below)
   Ice
2 spiral-cut grapefruit twists (p. 20), for garnish

In a cocktail shaker, combine the grapefruit juice, lime juice, Honey Syrup and Allspice Syrup; fill the shaker with ice and shake well. Strain into a chilled, ice-filled collins glass and garnish with the grapefruit twists.

ALLSPICE SYRUP

In a spice grinder, coarsely grind 1 tablespoon allspice berries. In a small saucepan, combine the ground allspice with 8 ounces water and bring to a boil. Remove from the heat, cover and let stand for 20 minutes. Pour through a fine strainer into a jar. Add 1 cup sugar, cover and shake gently until dissolved. Refrigerate for up to 1 month. Makes about 12 ounces. —*Jennifer Colliau*

Fuji Apple Soda

●◐● | ▌| Makes: **1**

Time: **10 min** plus overnight steeping

This drink arose from "a nerdy, geeked-out sommelier monologue," says Sean Beck of Back-street Café in Houston. To test the sommelier's long-winded pro-nouncement that Fuji apples are the best, Beck tried eight apple varieties.

3 ounces chilled club soda
2 ounces Apple-Ginger Syrup (below)
   Ice
2 apple slices, for garnish

In a chilled highball glass, combine the club soda and Apple-Ginger Syrup; fill with ice, stir well and garnish.

APPLE-GINGER SYRUP

In a jar, combine 16 ounces apple juice (preferably Fuji), ⅓ cup honey and 4 teaspoons chopped fresh ginger; refrigerate overnight. Strain into a container and add 5 ounces cranberry juice. Refrigerate the syrup for up to 1 week. Makes about 22 ounces. *—Sean Beck*

Bee's Ease

●◐● | ▪ | Makes: **1**

Time: **5 min** plus steeping and cooling

Lynnette Marrero, owner of Drinks at 6 cocktail catering and consulting company, created this refreshing virgin take on the gin-based Bee's Knees. She sweetens lavender-mint iced tea with a pale, floral acacia honey syrup.

2 ounces Lavender-Mint Tea (below)
1 ounce fresh lemon juice
¾ ounce Honey Syrup (p. 22)
   Ice
1 ounce chilled club soda
1 mint sprig, for garnish

In a cocktail shaker, combine the tea, lemon juice and Honey Syrup; fill with ice and shake well. Strain into a chilled rocks glass, stir in the club soda and garnish.

LAVENDER-MINT TEA

In a saucepan, bring 12 ounces water to a low simmer. Remove from the heat and add 1 tablespoon dried lavender buds and 3 mint sprigs; let steep for 5 minutes. Strain into a jar; let cool. Refrigerate for up to 24 hours. Makes 11 ounces. *—Lynnette Marrero*

Free Jamaica

2 **tablespoons dried hibiscus flowers or loose hibiscus tea**

1 **ounce fresh lime juice**

½ **ounce fresh ginger juice (from a 2-inch piece of ginger, grated and pressed through a fine strainer)**

½ **ounce Rich Simple Syrup (p. 22)**

   Crushed ice (p. 21)

1 or 2 **mint sprigs, for garnish**

1. In a small saucepan, bring 4 ounces of water to a boil. Remove from the heat, add the hibiscus flowers and let steep for 20 minutes. Strain the tea and let cool completely.

2. In a chilled collins glass, combine the lime juice, ginger juice and Rich Simple Syrup. Add crushed ice. Spin a swizzle stick or bar spoon between your hands to mix the drink, then add more crushed ice. Stir in the cooled hibiscus tea, garnish with mint sprigs and serve with a metal spoon-straw. — *Thad Vogler*

●●● | ▮ | Makes: **1**

Time: **10 min** plus steeping and cooling

Fresh ginger juice replaces the usual rum in this tasty, teetotaling Queen's Park Swizzle. Hibiscus tea, sold as *flor de Jamaica* in Latin markets, gives the drink a red tint.

Fighter's Reprieve

2 **ounces fresh orange juice**

½ **teaspoon cherry preserves**

½ **teaspoon barley malt syrup (molasses-like sweetener available at *edenfoods.com*.)**

2 **cracked black peppercorns**

Ice

In a cocktail shaker, combine the orange juice, cherry preserves, malt syrup and peppercorns; fill the shaker with ice and shake well. Fine-strain (p. 21) into a chilled coupe. — *Lydia Reissmueller*

●●● | ▼ | Makes: **1**

Barley malt syrup and cherry preserves contribute depth, sweetness and complexity to this nonalcoholic take on the Blood & Sand.

El Diablo Sobrio

●●● | ▌ | Makes: **1**

Sean Kenyon created "The Sober Devil" when a regular at his Denver bar, Williams & Graham, got pregnant. "She loved it so much, she said that she'd name the baby after me. She didn't."

6 **pink peppercorns**
½ **lime, cut into quarters**
5 **blackberries**
6 **ounces chilled ginger beer**
  Ice
1 **lime wheel, for garnish**

In a mixing glass, muddle the peppercorns, lime quarters and 4 blackberries with 2 ounces of the ginger beer. Fine-strain (p. 21) into a chilled, ice-filled collins glass, then stir in the remaining ginger beer. Garnish with the remaining blackberry and the lime wheel. —*Sean Kenyon*

Antilles Tea

●●● | ▌ | Makes: **1**

Time: **10 min** plus steeping | 📷 p. 214

"I like using tea as a base for nonalcoholic drinks," says San Francisco mixologist Jennifer Colliau. "It provides bitterness and more complexity than juice alone." Here, lemongrass tisane provides those qualities without caffeine.

2 **ounces chilled brewed lemongrass tea**
1 **ounce Clove Syrup (below)**
1 **ounce fresh lime juice**
  Ice
1 **lime wheel studded with cloves, for garnish**

In a cocktail shaker, combine the tea, Clove Syrup and lime juice; fill the shaker with ice and shake well. Strain into a chilled, ice-filled collins glass and garnish with the clove-studded lime wheel.

CLOVE SYRUP

In a spice grinder, coarsely grind 1½ teaspoons whole cloves. In a small saucepan, combine the ground cloves with 8 ounces water and bring to a boil. Remove from the heat, cover and let stand for 20 minutes. Pour through a fine strainer into a jar. Add 1 cup sugar, cover and shake gently until dissolved. Refrigerate for up to 1 month. Makes about 12 ounces. —*Jennifer Colliau*

EL DIABLO
SOBRIO
Glass by Deborah
Ehrlich.

Luchador's Daughter

●●● | ▮ | Makes: 1

Time: **20 min**

plus cooling

Caramelized-pineapple syrup sweetens hibiscus tea in this colorful, frothy drink from Momofuku bar director John deBary. Any left-over syrup would be fantastic drizzled over vanilla ice cream.

1½ ounces chilled brewed hibiscus tea
1 ounce fresh lime juice
1 ounce Caramelized-Pineapple Syrup (below)
1 large egg white
Ice
2 ounces chilled club soda
Pinch of cinnamon, for garnish

In a cocktail shaker, combine the hibiscus tea, lime juice, Caramelized-Pineapple Syrup and egg white and shake vigorously. Fill the shaker with ice and shake again. Strain into a chilled highball glass, stir in the club soda and garnish with the cinnamon.
—*John deBary*

CARAMELIZED-PINEAPPLE SYRUP

In a small skillet, toast ½ cinnamon stick until fragrant. In a small saucepan, combine 1 cup sugar, 4 ounces water, ¼ split vanilla bean and the toasted cinnamon. Cook without stirring until a light amber caramel forms, about 5 minutes. Reduce the heat and add 2½ cups chopped fresh pineapple. Simmer over moderately low heat until the pineapple softens, about 8 minutes. Discard the cinnamon stick and vanilla bean. Let the pineapple mixture cool slightly, then carefully pour into a blender and puree until smooth. Strain the syrup into a jar and let cool. Cover and refrigerate for up to 2 weeks. Makes about 8 ounces. —*Julian Cox*

Hot Buttered Lemon

2 **tablespoons unsalted butter**
2 **ounces fresh lemon juice**
2 **ounces hot water**
½ **ounce Simple Syrup (p. 22)**
1 **orange wedge**
1 **lemon wheel**
   Pinch of freshly grated nutmeg
   Pinch of cinnamon

In a small saucepan, melt the butter in the lemon juice over moderate heat. Add the hot water, Simple Syrup, orange wedge, lemon wheel, nutmeg and cinnamon and cook, stirring, until cloudy and hot. Pour into a small heatproof glass or warmed mug. —*Sebastian Reaburn*

 ● | ● | Makes: **1**

Sebastian Reaburn of The Lui Bar in Melbourne, Australia, describes this drink as a hot buttered rum crossed with a lemon tart. "The citrus gets softened by the heat and mellowed by the sugar and butter," he says. "It's delicious to nibble on at the end of the drink."

Five Spice

2 **ounces chilled brewed sweetened chai**
1 **ounce milk**
1 **teaspoon pure maple syrup**
½ **teaspoon pure vanilla extract**
2 **dashes of Angostura bitters (see Note)**
1 **large egg white**
   Ice
   Pinch of freshly grated nutmeg, for garnish

In a cocktail shaker, combine all of the ingredients except ice and the nutmeg and shake vigorously. Fill the shaker with ice and shake again. Strain the drink into a chilled coupe and garnish with the grated nutmeg. —*Julie Reiner*

Note The bitters are alcohol-based. For a completely nonalcoholic cocktail, leave them out.

● | ▼ | Makes: **1**

New York City mixologist Julie Reiner likes to serve the creamy, chai-based Five Spice as a holiday mocktail. "It has the holiday cheer without the booze," she says.

Bar Food

Trends of the decade ● Deviled eggs, tricked-out chicken wings and over-the-top burgers were big 10 years ago and became even more popular. ● Pork dominates the bar-food scene, from peanuts tossed with bacon bits (p. 178) to rich, bacon-infused pea crostini (p. 185). ● Spicy food reigns, as in fried chicken coated in chile sauce (p. 192) and ribs rubbed with loads of pepper (p. 200). ● As more people eat meals at the bar, bartenders create more and better cocktail-and-food pairings.

JACK ROSE, P. 124

MAPLE-GLAZED
PEANUTS &
BACON, P. 178

Maple-Glazed Peanuts & Bacon

Makes: **4 cups**

Active: **15 min**

Total: **1 hr** | 📷 p. 177

Sweet, salty and a little spicy, these beer nuts are from Meg Grace Larcom, chef-owner of The Redhead in New York City. The restaurant sells them online (*theredheadnyc.com*) in small zip pouches or 1-pound bags.

3   **thick slices of bacon (3 ounces)**
1   **tablespoon thyme leaves, minced**
1   **tablespoon kosher salt**
¾ **teaspoon Old Bay Seasoning**
½ **teaspoon cayenne pepper**
½ **teaspoon dry mustard**
3   **cups unsalted roasted peanuts (1 pound)**
½ **cup pure maple syrup**

1. Preheat the oven to 325°. In a medium skillet, cook the bacon over moderate heat until crisp, about 6 minutes. Transfer the bacon to paper towels to drain, then finely chop.

2. In a medium bowl, mix the thyme, salt, Old Bay, cayenne and dry mustard. Add the peanuts, maple syrup and bacon and toss until the peanuts are evenly coated. Scrape the nuts onto a parchment paper–lined baking sheet and roast for about 30 minutes, stirring once, until the maple syrup has thickened. Let the peanuts cool completely, stirring frequently to break up any large clumps. Serve the peanuts in glass jars or a large bowl.

—*Meg Grace Larcom*

Make Ahead The peanuts can be stored in an airtight container for up to 5 days.

Pimento Cheese

3 medium red bell peppers
5 ounces sharp yellow cheddar cheese,
   coarsely shredded (2 cups)
4 ounces cream cheese (½ cup), softened
¼ cup mayonnaise
1 tablespoon juice from a jar of bread-
   and-butter pickles (optional)
¼ teaspoon Tabasco
   Kosher salt and
   freshly ground pepper
   Saltine crackers, for serving

Makes: **6 servings**

Total: **30 min** plus

2 hr chilling

Atlanta chef Linton Hopkins became a pimento cheese convert when he tried his wife's recipe. "The sharpness of the cheddar cuts through the mayo so you get a more dynamic flavor," he says. Hopkins insists on roasting his own peppers and then mixing in the charred bits.

1. Roast the peppers directly over a gas flame or under a preheated broiler, turning, until charred all over. Transfer the peppers to a bowl, cover with plastic wrap and let steam for 15 minutes. Peel, seed and stem the peppers, then cut them into ⅛-inch dice; pat dry with paper towels.

2. In a medium bowl, mix the diced peppers with the cheddar, cream cheese, mayonnaise, pickle juice and Tabasco and season with salt and pepper. Cover and refrigerate for at least 2 hours. Serve with crackers. *—Linton Hopkins*

Make Ahead The Pimento Cheese can be refrigerated for up to 4 days.

Tuna Tartare Crisps

Makes: **8 servings**

Total: **40 min**

A hybrid of tuna tartare and tuna-avocado sushi rolls, these crisps from chef Lee Hefter get an extra punch of flavor from pickled ginger and wasabi mayo. Here, the tartare is served on baguette toasts; at CUT in Las Vegas, Hefter spoons it on potato chips.

32 thin baguette slices, cut from a medium loaf
¼ cup mayonnaise
1 teaspoon wasabi paste
   Kosher salt and freshly ground pepper
½ pound sushi-grade tuna, cut into ¼-inch dice
3 tablespoons soy sauce
1 Hass avocado, cut into ¼-inch dice
⅓ cup finely diced seedless cucumber
1 scallion, thinly sliced
2 teaspoons chopped pickled ginger

1. Preheat the oven to 350°. Toast the baguette slices on a large baking sheet until light golden and crisp, about 15 minutes. Let cool.

2. In a small bowl, mix the mayonnaise with the wasabi paste and season with salt and pepper.

3. In a medium bowl, gently mix the tuna with the soy sauce, avocado, cucumber, scallion and ginger. Spoon a dollop of the wasabi mayonnaise onto each toast, top with the tuna tartare and serve. —*Lee Hefter*

COSMOPOLITAN, P. 48

TUNA TARTARE
CRISPS

Buffalo Fried Pickles

Makes: **4 servings**

Total: **20 min**

Diners at Second Bar + Kitchen in Austin crave these fried pickles. According to chef David Bull, the bar snacks have just the right ratio of breading to pickle. "Plus, we serve them with a pretty intense Gorgonzola dip, which doesn't hurt either," he says.

Vegetable oil, for frying

2　kosher dill pickles (about 6 inches long), sliced lengthwise ¼ inch thick

All-purpose flour, for dredging

2　large eggs beaten with 2 tablespoons water

1　cup fine dry bread crumbs mixed with

1　teaspoon cayenne pepper

Blue cheese salad dressing and hot sauce, for serving

1. In a large saucepan, heat 1½ inches of oil to 375°. Pat the pickle slices dry with paper towels. Put the flour, eggs and bread crumbs in 3 separate shallow bowls. Dredge the pickle slices in flour, shaking off the excess. Dip them in the egg, then coat with the bread crumbs.

2. Fry the pickles, about 5 slices at a time, turning once, until browned and crisp, about 1 minute. Transfer to paper towels to drain. Serve hot, with blue cheese dressing and hot sauce. *—David Bull*

Guacamole with Pickled Jalapeños

Makes: **4 to 6 servings**

Total: **15 min**

Alex Stupak of NYC's Empellón offers this tip for the best-ever guacamole: "Don't overmash; you should see two shades of green in the avocado. If not, you've lost the texture."

2　Hass avocados, halved and pitted

¼　cup chopped cilantro

3　tablespoons minced white onion

2　pickled jalapeños, stemmed and finely chopped

1　tablespoon fresh lime juice

Sea salt

Tortilla chips, for serving

In a bowl, coarsely mash the avocados with a fork. Fold in the cilantro, onion, jalapeños and lime juice and season with salt. Serve with chips. *—Alex Stupak*

BUFFALO FRIED
PICKLES

Pommes Frites

Makes: **4 servings**

Active: **30 min**

Total: **1 hr 15 min**

Jonathon Sawyer's twice-fried pommes frites are legendary at The Greenhouse Tavern in Cleveland. Now they're served at the chef's newest venue, Sawyer's Street Frites at First Energy football stadium. The menu there includes the classic garlic-rosemary recipe here as well as carbonara, salt-and-vinegar and mozzarella-and-gravy frites.

2 **pounds baking potatoes, peeled and cut into ¼-inch-thick sticks**
   Vegetable oil, for frying
4 **garlic cloves, crushed**
1 **tablespoon finely chopped rosemary**
   Salt
   Dijon mustard, for serving

1. In a medium bowl, cover the potato sticks with water and let stand for 15 minutes. Drain, then rinse the potatoes and pat thoroughly dry.

2. In a large saucepan, heat 2 inches of vegetable oil to 275°. Line a baking sheet with paper towels. Working in batches, fry the potatoes until almost tender and slightly translucent, about 5 minutes. Transfer the potatoes to the paper towels to drain. Refrigerate for 30 minutes.

3. Reheat the oil to 350°. In a mortar, pound the garlic with the rosemary and a pinch of salt until a paste forms. Fry the potatoes in batches until golden and crisp, about 5 minutes. Using a slotted spoon, transfer the fries to a large rimmed baking sheet and immediately season with salt. Toss with the garlic-rosemary paste and serve the fries right away, with Dijon mustard alongside. —*Jonathon Sawyer*

Minty Peas & Bacon on Toast

1   **cup frozen peas, thawed**
2   **tablespoons unsalted butter, softened**
2   **tablespoons cream cheese, softened**
¼   **cup lightly packed mint leaves,
    plus chopped mint for garnish**
    Kosher salt
    Cayenne pepper
Four **½-inch-thick slices of sourdough bread**
    **Extra-virgin olive oil, preferably fruity,
    for brushing and garnish**
12   **thin bacon slices (6 ounces)**

1. Preheat the oven to 400°. In a food processor, combine the peas with the butter, cream cheese and the ¼ cup of mint. Pulse until nearly smooth; season the pea butter with salt and cayenne.

2. Brush the bread with olive oil and arrange the slices on a rimmed baking sheet. Toast the bread in the oven for about 8 minutes, turning once, until lightly golden but still chewy in the center. Transfer the toasts to a work surface; leave the oven on.

3. Spread each toast with about ¼ cup of the pea butter and top with 3 slices of bacon. Arrange the toasts on the baking sheet and bake for about 10 minutes, until the bacon just starts to render. Turn on the broiler and broil the toasts 6 inches from the heat for about 3 minutes, until the bacon starts to brown. Garnish the toasts with olive oil and chopped mint and serve warm. —*Gregory Vernick*

Makes: **4 servings**
Total: **35 min**

At Vernick Food & Drink in Philadelphia, chef Gregory Vernick spreads sourdough toasts with an easy pea "butter" made from frozen peas, cream cheese and mint. He then drapes the toasts with thin slices of bacon and torches them until crispy. To get the same effect, home cooks can pop the toasts under the broiler.

Smoked Trout Deviled Eggs

Makes: **8 servings**

Total: **35 min**

The deviled eggs at New York City's Pegu Club are as stellar as the expertly made cocktails. It's the hickory-smoked trout and curry mayonnaise in the filling that elevate this cocktail party standby.

8　large hard-boiled eggs, peeled and halved lengthwise

4　ounces skinless smoked-trout fillet, flaked

¼　cup mayonnaise

1　tablespoon chopped parsley

½　teaspoon curry powder

　　Kosher salt and freshly ground pepper

1　tablespoon chopped salted roasted almonds

Scoop the yolks from 12 of the hard-boiled egg halves into a bowl. (Reserve the remaining yolks for another use.) Add the trout, mayonnaise, parsley and curry powder; season with salt and pepper. Mix well to break up the trout. Mound the filling in the egg whites and arrange on a platter. Garnish with the almonds and serve. —*Gavin Citron*

Bacon-Wrapped Cherry Peppers

Makes: **4 to 6 servings**

Total: **30 min**

These super-easy hors d'oeuvres from Bluestem in Kansas City, Missouri, are a spicy, cheesy riff on traditional devils on horseback (bacon-wrapped dates). They're perfect for parties because they can be prepped ahead of time.

6　jarred hot cherry peppers—halved through the stem, seeded, drained and patted dry

⅓　cup cream cheese, softened

12　thin bacon slices (6 ounces)

1. Preheat the oven to 350°. Stuff each cherry pepper half with a heaping teaspoon of cream cheese and wrap with a slice of bacon; secure with a toothpick.

2. Arrange the peppers in a large ovenproof skillet and cook over moderate heat, turning, until the bacon is browned, 12 to 15 minutes. Transfer the skillet to the oven; bake for 5 minutes, until the bacon is crisp and the cream cheese is hot. Serve warm. —*Colby Garrelts*

Nachos with Pinto Beans & Jack Cheese

Makes: **6 to 8 servings**

Total: **1 hr**

"Nachos are my dirty little secret snack," says San Francisco chef Traci Des Jardins. "They can be so delicious if you use great sturdy chips, freshly roasted chiles and a good salsa." They're a real crowd-pleaser at her two Mijita restaurants and Public House.

1 pound tomatoes
1 white onion, halved lengthwise
3 garlic cloves
2 chipotles in adobo sauce, stemmed
   Kosher salt and freshly ground pepper
3 poblano chiles
One 1-pound bag tortilla chips
1 pound Monterey Jack cheese, shredded
One 15-ounce can pinto beans, rinsed and drained
   Mexican *crema* or sour cream, guacamole, cilantro and minced white onion, for serving

1. Light a grill or preheat a grill pan. Grill the tomatoes, halved onion and garlic over moderately high heat, turning, until charred in spots, about 10 minutes. In a saucepan, simmer the tomatoes, onion, garlic and chipotles with 1½ cups of water over moderate heat until the onion is softened and the tomatoes burst, about 30 minutes. Transfer to a blender and puree until smooth. Season the salsa with salt and pepper.

2. Roast the poblanos over a gas flame, turning, until charred. Transfer to a bowl, cover with plastic and let steam for 15 minutes. Peel, seed and stem the chiles, then dice them.

3. Preheat the oven to 425°. Layer half of the chips on a foil-lined rimmed baking sheet. Scatter half of the cheese, beans and diced poblanos over the chips. Repeat the layering with the remaining chips, cheese, beans and poblanos. Drizzle half of the salsa on top and bake for about 10 minutes, until the cheese is melted. Drizzle *crema* over the nachos, top with guacamole and the remaining salsa, then sprinkle with cilantro and minced onion. Serve immediately.
—*Traci Des Jardins*

NACHOS WITH PINTO
BEANS & JACK CHEESE

Polpette in Spicy Tomato Sauce

Makes: **12 servings**
Active: **25 min** Total: **1 hr**

Ruggero Gadaldi serves these hearty veal-and-sausage meatballs at Beretta, his Italian comfort-food restaurant in San Francisco. They were inspired by the bold red-sauce cuisine on *The Sopranos*, one of Gadaldi's favorite TV shows.

- 1 pound ground veal
- ½ pound sweet Italian sausage, casings removed
- 1 cup dry bread crumbs
- ½ cup whole milk
- 3 garlic cloves, minced
- 2 tablespoons chopped flat-leaf parsley
- 2 large egg whites
- 1 tablespoon tomato paste
- ½ cup freshly grated Pecorino Romano cheese, plus more for sprinkling
  Salt and freshly ground pepper
- 2½ cups prepared tomato sauce
  Large pinch of crushed red pepper

1. Preheat the oven to 350°. In a large bowl, mix the veal with the sausage meat, bread crumbs, milk, garlic, chopped parsley, egg whites, tomato paste and ½ cup of pecorino; season with salt and pepper. Roll into 1½-inch meatballs. Bake the meatballs on a lightly oiled baking sheet for about 30 minutes, until browned and cooked through.

2. In a saucepan, season the tomato sauce with the crushed red pepper. Add the meatballs and simmer until the sauce is slightly thickened, about 8 minutes. Sprinkle with pecorino and serve. —*Ruggero Gadaldi*

Ike's Vietnamese Fish Sauce Wings

½ cup Asian fish sauce
½ cup superfine sugar
4 garlic cloves—2 crushed, 2 minced
3 pounds chicken wings, split at the drumettes
2 tablespoons vegetable oil, plus more for frying
1 cup cornstarch
1 tablespoon chopped cilantro
1 tablespoon chopped mint

Makes: **6 servings**
Total: **1 hr** plus **3 hr** marinating

1. In a large bowl, whisk the fish sauce, sugar and crushed garlic. Add the wings and toss to coat. Refrigerate for 3 hours, tossing the wings occasionally.

2. In a small skillet, heat the 2 tablespoons of oil. Add the minced garlic and cook over moderate heat until golden, about 3 minutes. Drain on paper towels.

3. In a large pot, heat 2 inches of oil to 350°. Pat the wings dry on paper towels; reserve the marinade. Spread the cornstarch in a shallow bowl, add the wings and turn to coat. Fry the wings in batches until golden and cooked through, about 10 minutes per batch. Drain on paper towels and transfer to a serving bowl.

4. In a small saucepan, simmer the marinade over moderately high heat until syrupy, about 5 minutes. Strain the sauce over the wings and toss. Top with the cilantro, mint and fried garlic and serve. —*Andy Ricker*

Customers wait for hours for these incredible wings at the Pok Pok locations in Portland, Oregon, and New York City. In the summer, the Portland restaurant goes through 3,500 pounds of wings a week. They're chef-owner Andy Ricker's re-creation of a popular drinking snack that he discovered at a Saigon *bia hoi* ("fresh beer") stand in 2001.

Chile-Marinated Fried Chicken

Makes: **4 servings**

Total: **1 hr** plus overnight marinating

Paul Qui is a self-confessed fried chicken fanatic. "When I was growing up in Manila, fried chicken was always a treat," says the chef-owner of Qui in Austin. The key to his version, he explains, is marinating the chicken in Red Boat fish sauce.

¾ cup Thai sweet chile sauce

½ cup plus 2 tablespoons Asian fish sauce

One 4-pound chicken, cut into 8 pieces

1 cup palm sugar or light brown sugar

¼ cup minced cilantro stems

1 tablespoon minced fresh lemongrass (tender inner core only)

1 tablespoon *sambal oelek* or other Asian hot chile sauce

1 cup cornstarch

Vegetable oil, for frying

1. In a large bowl, whisk ¼ cup of the sweet chile sauce with ¼ cup of water and 2 tablespoons of the fish sauce. Add the chicken and turn to coat. Cover and refrigerate overnight.

2. In a small saucepan, combine the remaining ½ cup of fish sauce with the palm sugar, cilantro, lemongrass and *sambal oelek.* Simmer over moderate heat until reduced to ½ cup, about 8 minutes. Strain the sauce through a fine strainer into a bowl. Stir in the remaining ½ cup of sweet chile sauce; let cool.

3. Spread the cornstarch in a shallow bowl. Remove the chicken from the marinade, scraping the excess back into the bowl. Dredge the chicken in the cornstarch.

4. In a large, deep skillet, heat 1 inch of oil to 350°. Fry the chicken at 300°, turning once, until the skin is golden and an instant-read thermometer inserted in the thickest part of each piece registers 160°, 15 to 18 minutes. Transfer the fried chicken to the sauce and toss to coat. Arrange the chicken on a platter and serve right away. —Paul Qui

CHILE-MARINATED
FRIED CHICKEN

Chicken & Poblano Tacos with Crema

Makes: **4 servings**

Total: **45 min**

To make these tacos extraordinary, Justin Large of Chicago's Big Star recommends roasting the poblanos over an open flame until they're charred and blistered all over. "Roasting the chiles adds an unbelievable depth and presence to the dish," he says.

5   poblano chiles

4   boneless chicken thighs with skin (1 pound), pounded ½ inch thick
    Extra-virgin olive oil, for brushing
    Kosher salt and freshly ground pepper

½   cup chopped cilantro

12   warm corn tortillas
    Mexican *crema* or sour cream, shredded romaine lettuce, chopped white onion and lime wedges, for serving

1. Roast the poblanos directly over a gas flame or under a preheated broiler, turning, until charred all over. Transfer the chiles to a bowl, cover with plastic wrap and let steam for 15 minutes. Peel, seed and stem the chiles, then cut them into ¼-inch strips.

2. Light a grill or preheat a grill pan. Brush the chicken all over with oil and season with salt and pepper. Grill over moderately high heat, turning once, until the skin is crisp and browned, about 8 minutes. Transfer the chicken to a carving board and cut into ½-inch strips.

3. In a medium bowl, toss the poblano strips with the chicken and cilantro and season with salt and pepper. Serve the chicken-poblano filling in the warm tortillas with the *crema*, lettuce, onion and lime wedges. —*Justin Large*

Danger Tots

Vegetable oil, for frying
One 32-ounce package frozen Tater Tots
    Kosher salt
1½ cups shredded sharp cheddar cheese
 ½ cup prepared guacamole
 ¼ cup sour cream
  3 slices of bacon, cooked until crisp and crumbled
  1 plum tomato—halved, seeded
     and cut into ¼-inch dice
  1 jalapeño, thinly sliced

Makes: **6 servings**

Total: **35 min**

Loaded with cheddar, bacon, sour cream and guacamole, these amped-up Tater Tots aren't on the menu at PDT in Manhattan, but insiders know to ask for them. The woman behind this over-the-top creation is Jane Danger, a former PDT bartender.

1. In a large, deep skillet, heat 1 inch of vegetable oil to 400°. Working in batches, fry the Tater Tots, stirring once or twice, until golden and crisp, about 3 minutes. Transfer to paper towels to drain and season with salt.

2. Preheat the broiler. Pile the fried Tater Tots on an ovenproof serving plate and sprinkle with the cheese. Broil 2 inches from the heat for about 1 minute, or until the cheese is melted. Spoon the guacamole and sour cream over the Tater Tots, sprinkle with the bacon, tomato and jalapeño and serve. —Jane Danger

Cubano Sandwiches

Makes: **4 servings**

Total: **45 min**

At The Spotted Pig in New York City, chef April Bloomfield layers her *cubano* with a salty, satisfying combo of prosciutto and Gruyère instead of the traditional ham and Swiss. And in place of the mayo that makes most *cubanos* ridiculously greasy, she spreads the bread with a tangy, mustardy relish that's flecked with chopped cornichons, pickled jalapeños and capers.

¾ cup cornichons, chopped, plus ½ tablespoon cornichon pickling liquid

¼ cup sliced pickled jalapeños, chopped

2 tablespoons drained capers, chopped

3 tablespoons Dijon mustard

4 large French bread rolls, split, or 1 large baguette, cut into 4 pieces

3 tablespoons extra-virgin olive oil

4 cups shredded Gruyère cheese (10 ounces)

2 pounds roasted pork, preferably shoulder, sliced ¼ inch thick

Kosher salt and freshly ground pepper

¼ pound thinly sliced prosciutto

1. Preheat the oven to 375°. In a small bowl, mix the cornichons and their pickling liquid with the jalapeños, capers and mustard.

2. Brush the outsides of the rolls with the oil and place each on a 12-inch piece of foil, cut side up. Sprinkle ½ cup of Gruyère over the bottom half of each roll. Top with the sliced pork. Spread ¼ cup of the cornichon mixture over the pork and season with salt and pepper. Top with the prosciutto and the remaining Gruyère. Close the sandwiches and tightly roll them up in foil. Bake for 20 minutes, until the cheese is melted and the rolls are crisp. Slice in half on the bias and serve. —*April Bloomfield*

CUBANO
SANDWICHES

Kogi Dogs

Makes: **8 servings**

Total: **40 min**

Bacon-wrapped "dirty dogs" have been a longtime staple for late-night diners in L.A. Chef Roy Choi, king of the Kogi food truck empire, thought it was time for an upgrade. "I wanted to dress mine to the nines with our best toppings: napa cabbage salad, kimchi and toasted-sesame mayo," he says. "Make sure to crisp out the hot dogs so there's a nice snap when you bite into them," he adds.

2   **cups finely shredded cabbage**
1   **large scallion, finely chopped**
1   **tablespoon fresh lime juice**
    Salt and freshly ground pepper
½   **cup mayonnaise**
1   **tablespoon toasted sesame seeds, crushed**
1   **tablespoon vegetable oil, plus more for brushing**
1   **cup kimchi, drained and patted dry**
8   **hot dog buns**
8   **all-beef hot dogs, partially split**
1   **cup shredded sharp cheddar cheese**
2   **cups shredded romaine lettuce**
1   **small onion, thinly sliced**
2   **cups cilantro sprigs**
    Sriracha, for drizzling

1. In a large bowl, toss the cabbage with the scallion and lime juice; season with salt and pepper. In a small bowl, mix the mayonnaise with the sesame seeds and season with salt.

2. In a medium nonstick skillet, heat the 1 tablespoon of oil. Add the kimchi and cook over high heat until browned, about 3 minutes.

3. Light a grill or preheat a grill pan. Brush the cut sides of the hot dog buns with oil and grill over moderately high heat until toasted on both sides, about 45 seconds total. Spread the cut sides of the buns with the sesame mayonnaise.

4. Grill the hot dogs over moderately high heat until nicely charred all over. Tuck them in the buns; top with the kimchi, cheddar, cabbage salad, lettuce, onion and cilantro. Drizzle with Sriracha and serve. —*Roy Choi*

Lola Burgers

8   thick-cut slices of smoky bacon (½ pound)
1½ pounds mixed ground sirloin and chuck
     Kosher salt and freshly ground pepper
4   slices of smoked cheddar cheese (2 ounces)
4   large eggs
4   English muffins, toasted
¼   cup pickled cocktail onions, thinly sliced
     Ketchup and mustard, for serving

1. In a large nonstick skillet, cook the bacon over moderate heat until crisp, about 6 minutes. Drain on paper towels. Pour off all but 1 tablespoon of the bacon fat in the skillet.

2. Preheat a grill pan. Shape the meat into four 5-inch patties and season generously with salt and pepper. Grill over moderately high heat until lightly charred, about 3 minutes. Flip the burgers and top with the smoked cheddar. Cook for about 3 minutes longer for medium-rare meat.

3. Meanwhile, in the reserved bacon fat in the skillet, fry the eggs over-easy over moderate heat, about 3 minutes. Set the burgers on the bottoms of the English muffins and top with the pickled onions, bacon and fried eggs. Close the burgers and serve with ketchup and mustard. —*Michael Symon*

Makes: **4 servings**

Total: **35 min**

This mash-up of a hamburger and breakfast sandwich is from star chef Michael Symon, whose Cleveland-area restaurant empire includes the B Spot burger chain. He piles a beef patty, smoked cheddar, bacon and an oozy fried egg on a toasted English muffin.

Blue Smoke Black Pepper Ribs

Makes: **8 servings**

Active: **10 min**

Total: **2 hr 45 min**

Inspired by barbecue joints in Texas, the peppery beef ribs served at Blue Smoke in Manhattan are replete with hickory smoke. The cheater's version here calls for easier-to-find pork ribs and pimentón de la Vera, smoked Spanish paprika.

2   **tablespoons coarsely ground pepper**

2   **tablespoons brown sugar**

1   **tablespoon kosher salt**

1   **teaspoon pimentón de la Vera**

2   **racks pork baby back ribs (about 4½ pounds)**

Preheat the oven to 350°. In a small bowl, mix the pepper with the sugar, salt and smoked paprika. Sprinkle both sides of the ribs with the pepper mixture. Place the ribs meaty side up on a large rimmed baking sheet and bake for 2½ hours, or until the meat begins to pull away from the bones. Transfer the ribs to a cutting board and let stand for 5 minutes. Cut the racks into individual ribs and serve. —*Blue Smoke*

BLUE SMOKE
BLACK
PEPPER RIBS

RUM RIVER
MYSTIC, P. 90

Top 100 Bars

Trends of the decade ● Speakeasy-style bars with hidden entrances and secret phone numbers become hyper-popular. ● Restaurants launch excellent cocktail programs, and superstar chefs like Grant Achatz open high-concept bars (The Aviary in Chicago, p. 206). ● Hotel bars, once synonymous with bad drinks, begin to employ top mixologists. ● Specialty bars focus on one spirit: Seven Grand in L.A. (whiskey), Smuggler's Cove in San Francisco (rum, p. 212).

THIS BUILDING CONST. 1828
IS ON THE
FRAUNCES TAVERN
BLOCK HISTORIC DISTRICT

The Dead Rabbit
Grocery and Grog
in New York City,
p. 204

East Coast

Boston

CITIZEN PUBLIC HOUSE & OYSTER BAR Along with craft cocktails, this bar outside Fenway Park offers a selection of over 200 whiskeys, with flights that change weekly. *1310 Boylston St.; 617-450-9000; citizenpub.com.*

DRINK This underground spot has three bars, each making a different style of cocktail. *348 Congress St.; 617-695-1806; drink fortpoint.com.*

THE HAWTHORNE At Jackson Cannon's homey lounge inside the Hotel Commonwealth, bartenders pour classic cocktails and innovative drinks. *500A Commonwealth Ave.; 617-532-9150; thehawthornebar.com.*

NO. 9 PARK Customers can choose from one of two drinks menus at this bar in star chef Barbara Lynch's flagship restaurant: light aperitifs and serious cocktails. *9 Park St.; 617-742-9991; no9park.com.*

New York City

ATTABOY Behind an unmarked door in the original Milk & Honey space is this new bar. There's no menu; mixologists make drinks based on your spirit preference. *134 Eldridge St., Manhattan; no phone.*

BOOKER AND DAX Dave Arnold, the mad scientist of molecular mixology, concocts liquid-nitrogen-chilled drinks at the back of Momofuku Ssäm Bar. *207 Second Ave., Manhattan; 212-254-3500; momofuku.com.*

THE BUTTERFLY Eben Freeman serves experimental cocktails at this Midwest-themed bar and supper club. *225 West Broadway, Manhattan; 646-692-4943; thebutterflynyc.com.*

CLOVER CLUB Master mixologist Julie Reiner runs this classic-cocktails venue anchored by a historic 1892 bar. *210 Smith St., Brooklyn; 718-855-7939; cloverclubny.com.*

THE DEAD RABBIT GROCERY AND GROG Jack McGarry and Sean Muldoon created this beautiful 1890s throwback with an upstairs parlor boasting a dozen drink categories—juleps and smashes, for instance. *30 Water St., Manhattan; 646-422-7906; deadrabbit nyc.com.*

DEATH & CO Some of today's top mixologists (Philip Ward, Alex Day) created the menu of over 50 seasonal cocktails. *433 E. Sixth St., Manhattan; 212-388-0882; deathandcompany.com.*

EMPLOYEES ONLY A stunning Prohibition-era interior provides the backdrop for creative cocktails at this established speakeasy. *510 Hudson St., Manhattan; 212-242-3021; employees onlynyc.com.*

FORT DEFIANCE At this café and bar in Red Hook, owner St. John Fritzell serves stellar cocktails like the King Bee: Comb honey vodka, Darjeeling tea, lemon and cava.

365 Van Brunt St., Brooklyn; 347-453-6672; fortdefiancebrooklyn.com.

THE LONG ISLAND BAR At this former greasy spoon, Toby Cecchini serves updated classics—like a lime-ginger cordial gimlet—in a '50s atmosphere. *110 Atlantic Ave., Brooklyn; 718-625-8908; thelongislandbar.com.*

MAISON PREMIERE This intimate, 1800s-style oyster bar and cocktail den has the largest collection of absinthes and absinthe cocktails in New York City. *298 Bedford Ave., Brooklyn; 347-335-0446; maisonpremiere.com.*

THE NOMAD Leo Robitschek's drinks at the bar in The NoMad Hotel feature house infusions, fresh produce and intriguing spices. *1170 Broadway, Manhattan; 212-796-1500; thenomadhotel.com.*

PDT A phone booth is the secret entrance to Jim Meehan's bar. Terrifically creative drinks are paired with hot dogs from the adjacent Crif Dogs. *113 Saint Marks Pl., Manhattan; 212-614-0386; pdtnyc.com.*

PEGU CLUB Founded by vintage cocktail guru Audrey Saunders, Pegu Club serves its drinks with dropper bottles of fresh juices, bitters and simple syrup. *77 W. Houston St., Manhattan; 212-473-7348; peguclub.com.*

POURING RIBBONS Joaquín Simó's menu plots drinks on a matrix based on four categories: refreshing, spiritous, comforting and adventurous. *225 Avenue B, Manhattan; 917-656-6788; pouringribbons.com.*

Philadelphia

1 TIPPLING PLACE A rotating list of barrel-aged cocktails and seasonal punches anchors the menu at this cozy mid-century-style parlor. *2006 Chestnut St.; 215-665-0456; 1tpl.com.*

EMMANUELLE This French-themed cocktail lounge features craft cocktails, plus well-chosen classics. *1052 N. Hancock St. #67; 267-639-2470; drink emmanuelle.com.*

THE FRANKLIN MORTGAGE & INVESTMENT CO. In a building that fronted the nation's largest alcohol-smuggling ring during Prohibition, this bar maintains a speakeasy feel. *112 S. 18th St.; 267-467-3277; thefranklinbar.com.*

Washington, DC Area

BARMINI Star chef José Andrés transforms the cocktail experience using cutting-edge techniques and ingredient combinations. The Veruka Salt (peanut-infused rum, pineapple grog, salted peanut crumbs) is a favorite. *855 E St. NW, Washington, DC; 202-393-4451; minibarbyjoseandres.com.*

COLUMBIA ROOM Just 12 blocks from the White House, Derek Brown's bar honors the art of cocktail making with house-made cordials, bitters and tinctures and hand-carved ice. *1021 Seventh St. NW, Washington, DC; 202-393-0336; passenger dc.com/columbia.*

THE EDDY BAR This apothecary-style cocktail joint inside Hank's Oyster Bar serves homemade sodas and unique cocktails. *633 Pennsylvania Ave. SE, Washington, DC; 202-733-1971; hanksoysterbar.com.*

PX Todd Thrasher oversees the bar program at this intimate 1920s-style speakeasy. *728 King St., Alexandria, VA; 703-299-8385; eamonnsdublin chipper.com.*

RANGE Order Chartreuse on tap or avant-garde cocktails at the long marble bar in chef Bryan Voltaggio's restaurant complex. *5335 Wisconsin Ave. NW, Washington, DC; 202-803-8020; voltrange.com.*

Midwest

Chicago

THE AVIARY Beverage director Charles Joly concocts extraordinary drinks at this molecular-mixology bar owned by star chef Grant Achatz. *955 W. Fulton Market; 312-226-0868; theaviary.com.*

THE BARRELHOUSE FLAT This watering hole has an extensive menu arranged by base spirit for stirred, shaken, bubbly or egg drinks. *2624 N. Lincoln Ave.; 773-857-0421; barrelhouseflat.com.*

SABLE KITCHEN & BAR Chef-turned-mixologist Mike Ryan oversees the "liquid library" of booze served at the 40-foot bar. The syrups, infusions, tinctures and bitters are made in-house. *505 N. State St.; 312-755-9704; sablechicago.com.*

SCOFFLAW Gin cocktails are the specialty at this neighborhood bar, many mixed with house-distilled Old Tom gin. *3201 W. Armitage Ave.; 773-252-9700; scofflawchicago.com.*

THREE DOTS AND A DASH With a nod to tiki cocktail legends of the past, Paul McGee has created a tropical oasis where rum is plentiful and drinks are served in Polynesian mugs. *435 N. Clark St.; 312-610-4220; threedots chicago.com.*

THE VIOLET HOUR This modern, stately bar offers fanciful, complex cocktails, such as the gin-based Grizzley Eve, with Campari, orange marmalade, pineapple and grapefruit bitters. *1520 N. Damen Ave.; 773-252-1500; theviolethour.com.*

Wisconsin

BLUE JACKET This Great Lakes–inspired small-plates restaurant offers a daily grog and a great maple egg cream brunch cocktail. *135 E. National Ave., Milwaukee; 414-312-7098; bluejacketbar.com.*

BRYANT'S COCKTAIL LOUNGE
Aside from the fish tank
and vintage McIntosh
stereo, Bryant's looks like
it hasn't changed at all
since it opened in 1938.
*1579 S. Ninth St., Milwau-
kee; 414-383-2620;
bryantscocktaillounge.com.*

MERCHANT By day a liquor
shop, at night the bar/
restaurant serves a sea-
sonal selection of drinks,
like a spiked root beer
float sweetened with
house-made cardamom-
chocolate syrup. *121 S.
Pinckney St., Madison;
608-259-9799; merchant
madison.com.*

Minneapolis

BRADSTREET CRAFTSHOUSE
Toby Maloney's novel
drinks like the Smoked
Brinner (bourbon, Laga-
vulin Scotch, maple syrup,
bacon and bitters) are
served in one of four
seating areas: the chef's
counter, main bar, parlor
or dining room. *601 N.
First Ave.; 612-312-1821;
bradstreetcraftshouse.com.*

EAT STREET SOCIAL The
soda-fountain drinks at
this American bistro-bar

are nostalgic, such as the
Merry Widow (banana
cream, egg and Dutch
chocolate syrup). *18 W.
26th St.; 612-767-6850;
eatstreetsocial.com.*

MARVEL BAR Basic ingredients like salt add subtle
complexity to drinks
here. Bartender's choice
is The Gatsby, a decep-
tively simple Scotch
drink, watered down
and served neat. *50 N.
Second Ave.; 612-206-
3929; marvelbar.com.*

Missouri

**MANIFESTO AT THE RIEGER
HOTEL GRILL & EXCHANGE**
This underground
hideaway feels like a
neighborhood bar but
serves ambitious drinks.
*1924 Main St., Kansas City;
816-536-1325; theriegerkc.
com/manifesto.*

PLANTER'S HOUSE
Among the dozens of
cocktails are original
drinks by Ted Kilgore,
classics and riffs on classics, like the Manhat-
tanite: rye, vermouth,
Suze and chocolate

bitters. *1000 Mississippi
Ave., St. Louis; 314-696-
2603; plantershousestl.com.*

TASTE The short drinks
list is perfect for the
indecisive drinker. It's
broken down by flavor
profile, with just four
offerings for each. *4584
Laclede Ave., St. Louis; 314-
361-1200; tastebarstl.com.*

South

Louisville

PROOF ON MAIN
A rotating collection of
artwork lines the walls
of this bar adjoining the
21C Museum Hotel.
In addition to cocktails,
there are more than
75 Kentucky bourbons
and excellent microbrews.
*702 W. Main St.; 502-217-
6360; proofonmain.com.*

THE SILVER DOLLAR With
Bakersfield Sound tunes
playing over the speak-
ers and an unbeatable
collection of Kentucky
whiskeys, this honky-
tonk pays homage to the
great juke joints of the
past. *1761 Frankfort Ave.;
502-259-9540; whiskey
bythedrink.com.*

Nashville

HUSK Housed in a charming mansion, this bar-restaurant operates on a strict Southern-ingredient-only policy. Sip the bright, caraway-inflected Rye Rocket on the porch overlooking the city. *37 Rutledge St.; 615-256-6565; husknashville.com.*

THE PATTERSON HOUSE It's not unlikely you'll find a celebrity or two among the crowd at this bar below The Catbird Seat (Jack White has made a visit here). *1711 Division St.; 615-636-7724; thepattersonnashville.com.*

ROLF AND DAUGHTERS The well-rounded bar program at this Italian restaurant offers tasty cocktails like the Red Herring: vodka, cherry Heering, lime and Cabernet Sauvignon. *700 Taylor St.; 615-866-9897; rolfanddaughters.com.*

Atlanta Area

H. HARPER STATION This long, narrow bar in an old railroad freight depot specializes in punch, served in crystal bowls. *904 Memorial Dr., Atlanta; 678-732-0415; hharperstation.com.*

HOLEMAN & FINCH Chef Linton Hopkins redefined Atlanta's food and drink scene with this gastropub. Try a Roy's Robe, a smoky, spiced winter cocktail served over a single large ice cube. *2277 Peachtree Rd., Atlanta; 404-948-1175; holeman-finch.com.*

KIMBALL HOUSE Oysters and absinthe are the stars at this cozy neighborhood spot. There are plenty of cocktails to choose from too, like the Pecan Old-Fashioned. *303 E. Howard Ave., Decatur, GA; 404-378-3502; kimball-house.com.*

LEON'S FULL SERVICE Taking the lead from old-time full-service gas stations, the team here gives guests the total package: great food, a terrific waitstaff, a comfortable atmosphere and exciting drinks. *131 E. Ponce de Leon Ave., Decatur, GA; 404-687-0500; leonsfullservice.com.*

PAPER PLANE The restaurant's motto is "vintage service, modern fare." At the bar you'll find inventive cocktails like the bourbon-based About Last Night, with Madeira, honey and Pommeau de Normandie. *340 Church St., Decatur, GA; 404-377-9308; the-paper-plane.com.*

Charleston, South Carolina

THE BELMONT Exposed-brick walls line this rustic bar, where guests can snack on charcuterie and cheese alongside diverse cocktails like the spicy-sweet Brown Derby (bourbon, grapefruit and jalapeño-infused honey). *511 King St.; no phone; the belmontcharleston.com.*

FIG The cocktail menu at this locavore restaurant has three sections: proprietary drinks, Negroni riffs and Make Your Own Manhattan. *232 Meeting St.; 843-805-5900; eatatfig.com.*

THE GIN JOINT If you're the indecisive type, you can let the bartenders create your perfect drink or choose something from their line of Bittermilk bottled mixers. *182 E. Bay St.; 843-577-6111; theginjoint.com.*

Miami Beach

THE BROKEN SHAKER Bar Lab partners Gabriel Orta and Elad Zvi's 2012 Broken Shaker pop-up was so successful, they created a brick-and-mortar location in the Freehand Miami hostel. *2727 Indian Creek Dr.; 305-531-2727; thefreehand.com.*

THE REGENT COCKTAIL CLUB With live jazz and John Lermayer's well-executed drinks, this classic-cocktail lounge evokes the 1940s, when The Regent hotel opened. *1690 Collins Ave.; 305-673-0199; galehotel.com.*

New Orleans

ARNAUD'S FRENCH 75 BAR Chris Hannah mans the bar at this dapper, cigar-friendly spot inside Arnaud's, one of New Orleans's oldest and most venerated restaurants. *813 Rue Bienville; 504-523-5433; arnauds restaurant.com.*

CURE Proper attire is requested at this self-described "bastion of civility and sophistication," a pioneer of modern cocktails in the city. *4905 Freret St.; 504-302-2357; curenola.com.*

SOBOU Ti Martin's friendly saloon in the French Quarter's W Hotel serves bold, New Orleans–style cocktails, mostly variations on the classics. *310 Rue Chartres; 504-552-4095; sobounola.com.*

Houston

ANVIL BAR & REFUGE All the restored and hand-crafted decorations in Bobby Heugel's remodeled 1950s tire store have backstories the bartenders will be happy to share while you sip stellar cocktails. *1424 Westheimer Rd.; 713-523-1622; anvilhouston.com.*

CAPTAIN FOXHEART'S BAD NEWS BAR & SPIRITS LODGE When Justin Burrow opened this pubby cocktail bar, his aim was to leave out the pretension and revive the emphasis on service. *308 Main St.; no phone.*

THE PASTRY WAR This *mezcaleria* from Bobby Heugel pours exclusively small-batch tequilas and mezcals in a space reminiscent of a Mexican pueblo. Try the agave spirits served neat or in a margarita or sour. *310 Main St.; 713-226-7770; facebook.com/thepastrywar.*

San Antonio

THE BROOKLYNITE Named for the classic daiquiri variation, this comfortable cocktail parlor throws fun Tiki Tuesday parties. *516 Brooklyn Ave.; 210-444-0707; thebrooklynitesa.com.*

Austin

MIDNIGHT COWBOY
Unless the "vacancy" sign is lit up outside, reservations are required to enter this lively, luxurious bar. Drinks are prepared tableside by expert bartenders. *313 E. Sixth St.; 512-843-2715; midnight cowboymodeling.com.*

Dallas

THE STANDARD POUR
The menu offers adventurous cocktails like The Brimstone: whiskey, citrus spiced tea–infused vermouth, Bénédictine and root beer bitters. *2900 McKinney Ave.; 214-935-1370; tspdallas.com.*

Southwest

Tucson

SAINT HOUSE In a city with a tequila reputation, this rum bar stands out, specializing in daiquiris and serving more than 40 rums. *256 E. Congress St.; 520-207-7757; saint houserumbar.com.*

SCOTT & CO. Patrons sip seasonal craft cocktails like the gin-based Spanish Handshake (Punt e Mes and house-made pineapple soda) in this small, quiet bar off the 47 Scott restaurant. *49 N. Scott Ave.; 520-624-4747; 47scott.com.*

Las Vegas

SAGE Fresh ingredients elevate beverages at this chic bar. One to try: A Distant Spring, with gin, lemon, raspberry syrup, rose and orange ice cubes. *3730 Las Vegas Blvd.; 702-590-8690; aria.com.*

VESPER BAR This 24-hour spot in The Cosmopolitan hotel offers a sophisticated escape from the Strip's casino buzz. On the menu you'll find classic cocktails opposite Vesper's spins on those drinks. *3708 Las Vegas Blvd.; 702-698-7000; cosmopolitanlasvegas.com.*

West Coast

San Diego

NOBLE EXPERIMENT
The stacked "kegs" next to the bathroom in the Neighborhood restaurant are actually the doorway to Noble Experiment; reservations (available by text request) required. The eight-drink menu offers cocktails like the Morning Glory Fizz: Scotch, lemon, sugar, egg white and absinthe. *777 G St.; 619-888-4713; nobleexperimentsd.com.*

POLITE PROVISIONS Behind the bar at Erick Castro's old apothecary–style bar is a long line of taps. Only a few spout beer— the rest pour craft sodas, select spirits like Lillet rosé and sherry and even coffee and draft cocktails. *4696 30th St.; 619-677-3784; politeprovisions.com.*

Los Angeles Area

BESTIA Rustic Italian food and serious cocktails like the White Negroni (gin, Kina L'Avion d'Or and

Suze) converge at this industrial-chic restaurant. *2121 Seventh Pl., L.A.; 213-514-5724; bestiala.com.*

COPA D'ORO The cocktail selection from Vincenzo Marianella begins with a "market menu," which lists a variety of spirits, herbs, fruits, juices, vegetables and jams for a mix-and-match drink experience. *217 Broadway, Santa Monica, CA; 310-576-3030; copadoro.com.*

HARVARD & STONE Some nights this is a low-key bar; other nights you'll find local rock 'n' roll bands playing while burlesque dancers perform. *5221 Hollywood Blvd, L.A.; 323-466-6063; harvardandstone.com.*

NO VACANCY Beyond one of the coolest entrances of any bar (we won't spoil the surprise) is a space reminiscent of the Moulin Rouge. The drinks menu is created by a rotating cast of a dozen star mixologists. *1727 Hudson Ave., L.A.; 323-465-1902; novacancyla.com.*

THE ROGER ROOM Nothing but an old neon sign for psychic readings marks the entrance to this elegant speakeasy. Drinks range from an absinthe mojito to a cucumber-foam tequila cocktail. *370 La Cienega Blvd., West Hollywood, CA; 310-854-1300; therogerroom.com.*

SCOPA ITALIAN ROOTS Backlit bottles make the bar the focal point of this modern Italian restaurant. Drinks like the Bullocks Wilshire (bourbon, Demerara rum, Cynar, maraschino liqueur) pair well with the antipasto plates. *2905 Washington Blvd., Venice, CA; 310-821-1100; scopaitalianroots.com.*

THE SPARE ROOM This modern gaming lounge in the Hollywood Roosevelt hotel is stocked with classic board games and two vintage bowling lanes. Guests drink cocktails on cushiony leather and velvet seats. *7000 Hollywood Blvd., L.A.; 323-769-7296; spareroomhollywood.com.*

THE VARNISH Enter through a secret door at Cole's, the famous French dip restaurant, and you'll be handed Eric Alperin and Sasha Petraske's menu with a selection of five or six cocktails, plus an option for bartender's choice. *118 E. Sixth St., L.A.; 213-622-9999; 213nightlife .com/thevarnish.*

San Francisco Area

BAR AGRICOLE At this bar in a sleek, sustainably designed building with a beautiful patio, Thad Vogler obsesses over the drinks. One to try: the spicy-fruity Bourbon Old-Fashioned, mixed with house-made stone-fruit bitters. *355 11th St., San Francisco; 415-355-9400; baragricole.com.*

BOURBON & BRANCH Serving hand-numbered bourbons, obscure rums and tequilas and rare Scotches, this underground bar was ahead of the curve when it opened almost a decade ago. *501 Jones St., San Francisco; 415-346-1735; bourbonandbranch.com.*

COMSTOCK SALOON At Jonny Raglin and Jeff Hollinger's turn-of-the-century-style saloon, customers can sample revived classics like pisco punch or the Barkeep's Whimsy, a.k.a. dealer's choice. *155 Columbus Ave., San Francisco; 415-617-0071; comstocksaloon.com.*

HARD WATER Whiskey aficionados will find a remarkable collection of the brown spirit here, including an extensive list of allocated and out-of-production bottles. *Pier 3, The Embarcadero, San Francisco; 415-392-3021; hardwaterbar.com.*

PRIZEFIGHTER With a decidedly pared-down drinks menu, this unadorned, unpretentious bar serves cocktails containing just three ingredients. *6702 Hollis St., Emeryville, CA; no phone; prizefighterbar.com.*

SMUGGLER'S COVE More than just a tiki bar, Martin Cate's pirate ship–themed bar celebrates the past, present and future of rum with cocktails by barman Marcovaldo Dionysos. *650 Gough St., San Francisco; 415-869-1900; smugglerscovesf.com.*

Portland, Oregon

CLYDE COMMON Jeffrey Morgenthaler, a pioneer of the barrel-aged cocktail movement, manages the bar at this gastropub. The food is as excellent as the drinks. *1014 SW Stark St.; 503-228-3333; clydecommon.com.*

MULTNOMAH WHISKEY LIBRARY Vested bartenders climb up brass ladders to grab liquors from shelves holding more than 1,500 bottles. The staff helps navigate the inventory via cocktails made tableside, spirits tastings and pairing dinners. *1124 SW Alder St.; 503-954-1381; mwlpdx.com.*

OVEN AND SHAKER Pies at Ryan Magarian's neighborhood pizzeria are served with cocktails like A Nap for Sasquatch: Cynar, grapefruit juice and ale with house-blend maple syrup. *1134 NW Everett St.; 503-241-1600; ovenandshaker.com.*

TEARDROP COCKTAIL LOUNGE Daniel Shoemaker uses house-made ingredients like marshmallow root tincture in drinks such as the Borrowed Time (tequila, blood orange, amaro, Chartreuse and bitters). *1015 NW Everett St.; 503-445-8109; teardroplounge.com.*

THE WOODSMAN TAVERN The whiskey-forward cocktail menu here reflects Portland's quirky personality. Drinks use only quality products screened by owner Duane Sorenson of Stumptown Coffee Roasters. *4537 SE Division St.; 971-373-8264; woodsmantavern.com.*

Seattle

CANON Jamie Boudreau curated a collection of over 2,800 spirits—the largest in the Western Hemisphere. Patrons can sample them in cocktails like the Oaxacan Scaffa (mezcal, Punt e Mes and maraschino liqueur), aged for nine months in a bourbon cask. *928 12th Ave.; 206-552-9755; canonseattle.com.*

ROB ROY A reel-to-reel tape deck and a record player occupy the back of this dimly lit bar serving small plates and delicious seasonal drinks. *2332 Second Ave.; 206-956-8423; robroyseattle.com.*

TAVERN LAW Locals love this bar for two reasons: its serious cocktail program and the killer burger topped with red wine onion jam, provolone and pork belly. *1406 12th Ave.; 206-322-9734; tavernlaw.com.*

ZIG ZAG CAFÉ On a quest to revive vintage cocktails, the team here uses quirky recipes from old cocktail guides as inspiration for drinks like Don't Give Up the Ship: gin, Dubonnet, Fernet-Branca and orange liqueur. 1501 Western Ave. #202; 206-625-1146; zigzagseattle.com.

Rocky Mountains

Colorado

GREEN RUSSELL This underground bar is decorated with antique lanterns and mirrors. For the best experience, let the bartenders tailor-make something for you. *1422 Larimer St., Denver; 303-893-6505; greenrussell.com.*

JIMMY'S The star of this Aspen institution is tequila, owner Jimmy Yeager's favorite spirit. Margaritas like the cranberry-and-mezcal Smokey draw on the selection of 120-plus tequilas and mezcals. *205 S. Mill St., Aspen; 970-925-6020; jimmysaspen.com.*

JUSTICE SNOW'S Part of the iconic Wheeler Opera House was transformed into this sleek restaurant and bar, which still retains an old-timey charm. In addition to cocktails, there are tableside punch bowls and traditional absinthe fountains.

328 E. Hyman Ave., Aspen; 970-429-8192; justice snows.com.

OAK AT FOURTEENTH The creative drinks by Bryan Dayton include novel house-made sodas like strawberry–kaffir lime and delicious low-proof cocktails as well as boozier concoctions. *1400 Pearl St., Boulder; 303-444-3622; oakat fourteenth.com.*

WILLIAMS & GRAHAM Bartenders at this speakeasy hidden behind a moving bookcase mix extraordinary cocktails like the Blackberry Sage Smash, with bourbon and lemon. *3160 Tejon St., Denver; 303-997-8886; williams andgraham.com.*

Wyoming

THE ROSE At this classically inspired cocktail lounge, perch on a black leather stool at the glossy wooden bar and order a Seared In Memory: Scotch, rum, Pernod and roasted pineapple. *50 W. Broadway Ave., Jackson Hole; 307 733-1500; therosejh.com.*

ANTILLES TEA, P. 172
Tall glass by Deborah Ehrlich.

Recipe Index

PAGE NUMBERS IN **BOLD** INDICATE PHOTOGRAPHS.

Barware Guide

Contributors

TONY ABOU-GANIM is a Las Vegas–based spirits expert.

ERIK ADKINS is the bar director for the San Francisco–based Slanted Door Group.

BRIDGET ALBERT currently serves as general secretary for the Illinois chapter of the US Bartenders' Guild.

SCOTT BEATTIE is a partner at Goose & Gander in Napa Valley.

SEAN BECK is the sommelier and beverage director at Backstreet Café, Caracol and Hugo's, all in Houston.

JULIO BERMEJO is the owner of Tommy's Mexican Restaurant in San Francisco.

JEFF BERRY has written five books on vintage tiki cocktails and cuisine, most recently *Beachbum Berry's Potions of the Caribbean*.

GREG BEST is an Atlanta-based bartender.

JACQUES BEZUIDENHOUT is the chief beverage consultant for Kimpton Hotels & Restaurants.

DYLAN BLACK is the owner of Green Street in Cambridge, Massachusetts.

JAMIE BOUDREAU is the owner of Canon in Seattle.

KAI BRAATEN created The Un-Usual Suspect cocktail (p. 60) at Canlis in Seattle.

LUCY BRENNAN is the owner of Mint and 820 in Portland, Oregon.

DEREK BROWN is a spirits writer and the owner of several bars in the DC area, including Mockingbird Hill.

JACKSON CANNON is the bar director at Island Creek Oyster Bar, Eastern Standard and The Hawthorne, which he also co-owns, all in Boston.

KATHY CASEY is a Seattle-based chef, mixologist and restaurant consultant with an online cocktail show called *Kathy Casey's Liquid Kitchen*.

ERICK CASTRO is a co-owner of Polite Provisions in San Diego.

MARTIN CATE owns Smuggler's Cove in San Francisco.

TOBY CECCHINI is a co-owner of Long Island Bar in Brooklyn, New York, and the author of *Cosmopolitan: A Bartender's Life*.

JENNIFER COLLIAU is the owner and producer of Small Hand Foods artisanal cocktail syrups and the bar manager at Long Now Salon in San Francisco.

WAYNE COLLINS developed and runs Mixxit, a bartender training program in the U.K.

JOHN COLTHARP is a Los Angeles–based bartender.

JULIAN COX is a co-owner of drink-focused Soigné Group consulting in Los Angeles.

BRYAN DAYTON is a co-owner of Oak at Fourteenth in Boulder, Colorado, and Acorn in Denver.

JOHN DEBARY is the bar director for the Momofuku restaurant group.

ROMÉE DE GORIAINOFF founded the Experimental Group, which includes the Experimental Cocktail Club in Paris, London and New York City.

DALE DEGROFF is a partner at the Beverage Alcohol Resource mixology training program and a cofounder of The Museum of the American Cocktail in New Orleans.

JOHN DERAGON heads the Cocktail Apprentice Program for the annual Tales of the Cocktail festival.

DEVLIN DEVORE KAPLAN is the bar manager at Jax Fish House & Oyster Bar in Boulder, Colorado.

MARCOVALDO DIONYSOS tends bar at Smuggler's Cove in San Francisco and co-owns H.M.S., a beverage catering service.

PHILIP DUFF co-owns Door 74, a speakeasy in Amsterdam, and Liquid Solutions, an international bar consulting company.

H. JOSEPH EHRMANN owns Elixir in San Francisco and founded Cocktail Ambassadors, a bar education and consulting network.

EFISIO FARRIS is the owner of Arcodoro in Houston.

KATHY FLICK collaborated with Marcovaldo Dionysos on creating the Ginger Rogers cocktail (p. 59).

EBEN FREEMAN, the director of bar operations and innovation for the Altamarea Group, runs the cocktails program at The Butterfly in New York City.

JOHN GERTSEN is the general manager and a bartender at Drink in Boston.

JEFF GRDINICH is the bar manager at The Rose in Jackson Hole, Wyoming.

CHRIS HANNAH is the mixologist at Arnaud's French 75 in New Orleans.

ZANE HARRIS tends bar at Evelyn in New York City.

MELISSA HAYES is a bartender at Leon's Full Service in Decatur, Georgia.

ROBERT HESS is the mixologist behind DrinkBoy.com and The Chanticleer Society.

BOBBY HEUGEL cofounded the hospitality group Clumsy Butcher, which includes Anvil Bar & Refuge, Underbelly and The Hay Merchant, all in Houston.

SEAN HOARD co-owns The Commissary, a provisions shop specializing in artisanal mixers in Portland, Oregon.

GREG HOITSMA is the head bartender at Andina in Portland, Oregon.

LINTON HOPKINS is the chef and co-owner of numerous restaurants in the Atlanta area, including Holeman & Finch Public House and Restaurant Eugene.

JOHNNY IUZZINI owns the pastry consulting company Sugar Fueled Inc.

DON JAVIER is the bartender and owner of La Capilla in Tequila, Mexico.

SEAN KENYON is the proprietor and barman at Williams & Graham in Denver.

EBEN KLEMM is a partner and cofounder of Cane & Maple food and beverage consulting company.

TOMMY KLUS is the bar manager at Multnomah Whiskey Library in Portland, Oregon.

NICK KOBBERNAGEL HOVIND runs the bar program at Ruby in Copenhagen.

IRA KOPLOWITZ & NICHOLAS KOSEVICH are cofounders of Bittercube, a Milwaukee-based artisanal bitters producer and cocktail consulting company.

TIM LACEY is a mixology consultant in Chicago.

FRANCESCO LAFRANCONI is the executive director of mixology and spirits educator for Southern Wine and Spirits of Nevada and founder of the Academy of Spirits and Fine Service.

DON LEE is the director of product development for Cocktail Kingdom, a purveyor of barware and cocktail ingredients.

JAMES LEE is a co-owner of The Bitter Bar in Boulder and the bar manager at Bōl in Vail, Colorado. He is also the owner of the forthcoming Lee & Bitters Co. restaurant in Austin.

JOHN LERMAYER is a bartender at The Regent Cocktail Club at the Gale Hotel in Miami Beach.

JASON LITTRELL founded and operates Critical Mass Events consulting firm in Brooklyn, New York.

KEVIN LUDWIG is a bartender at La Taq in Portland, Oregon.

PATRICIO MACIEL is a bartender at Bahía at the Four Seasons Hotel in Miami.

RYAN MAGARIAN cofounded Aviation American Gin and Oven and Shaker pizzeria and bar in Portland, Oregon.

TOBY MALONEY co-owns Pouring Ribbons in New York City, The Violet Hour in Chicago and The Patterson House in Nashville.

VINCENZO MARIANELLA is the head barman at Copa d'Oro in Santa Monica.

LYNNETTE MARRERO owns Drinks at 6, a cocktail catering and consulting firm.

NICK MAUTONE is a food-service consultant and author of *Raising the Bar: Better Drinks, Better Entertaining.*

DUGGAN MCDONNELL owns and distills Campo de Encanto pisco and tends bar at Cantina in San Francisco.

JACK MCGARRY created the drinks program for Manhattan's Dead Rabbit Grocery and Grog, where he is also a managing partner.

PAUL MCGEE is an associate partner at Lettuce Entertain You Enterprises in Chicago. He also created the bar program at Chicago's Three Dots and a Dash.

CHRIS MCMILLIAN runs the bar program at Kingfish in New Orleans.

JIM MEEHAN, *F&W Cocktails* deputy editor, is a co-owner of PDT in New York City.

JOSE MIRANDA is a former mixologist at WD-50 in New York City.

IVY MIX is a mixologist at Clover Club in Brooklyn, New York.

SEAN MULDOON is the founder and general manager of The Dead Rabbit Grocery and Grog in New York City.

LINDSAY NADER cofounded Elysium Craft Cocktail Services in Los Angeles.

BILL NORRIS is the beverage director of the Alamo Drafthouse, The Highball, 400 Rabbits and Midnight Cowboy, all in Austin.

SASHA PETRASKE is a cofounder of Milk & Honey and Little Branch in New York City.

JONNY RAGLIN is a partner at Comstock Saloon in San Francisco.

SEBASTIAN REABURN is the head bartender at The Lui Bar in Melbourne, Australia.

JULIE REINER co-owns Flatiron Lounge in Manhattan and Clover Club in Brooklyn.

LYDIA REISSMUELLER owns Tender Bar cocktail catering and consulting company in Portland, Oregon.

LEO ROBITSCHEK manages the bars at The NoMad Hotel and Eleven Madison Park in New York City.

JIM ROMDALL is the bar manager at Rumba in Seattle.

SAM ROSS is a co-owner of Attaboy cocktail bar in New York City.

MIKE RYAN is the head bartender at Sable Kitchen & Bar in Chicago.

JON SANTER is the owner and operator of Prizefighter bar in Emeryville, California.

AUDREY SAUNDERS founded Pegu Club in New York City.

ANTHONY SCHMIDT is the lead bartender for CH Projects in San Diego.

CRAIG SCHOETTLER oversees the spirits programs for the bars and restaurants at Aria Resort & Casino in Las Vegas.

FRANCIS SCHOTT is a co-owner of Stage Left and Catherine Lombardi restaurants in New Brunswick, New Jersey. He is also a co-host of *The Restaurant Guys* radio show.

JOSEPH SCHWARTZ is a co-owner of Little Branch in New York City.

GEORGE SCHWARZ is the owner of Temple Bar, The Noho Star, Keens Steakhouse and Elephant & Castle, all in New York City.

ADAM SEGER creates and manages the cocktail program for iPic Theaters.

DANIEL SHOEMAKER is a bartender and co-owner of Teardrop Cocktail Lounge in Portland, Oregon.

JOAQUÍN SIMÓ is a partner at Alchemy Consulting and a co-owner of Pouring Ribbons in New York City.

MATHIAS SIMONIS, a member of The Bon Vivants, a cocktail and spirits consulting company, tends bar at Trick Dog in San Francisco.

ERIC SIMPKINS is the beverage director and general manager at The Lawrence in Atlanta.

CHAD SOLOMON cofounded Cuffs & Buttons, a beverage consulting and catering company in New York City.

SØREN KROGH SØRENSEN is the owner of Ourselves Alone in Copenhagen.

RAY SRP is a bartender at Hakkasan in Las Vegas.

MURRAY STENSON is a Seattle-based bartender, most recently at Il Bistro.

JOEL TEITELBAUM is the portfolio ambassador for the Artisanal Group at Southern Wine & Spirits.

WILL THOMPSON tends bar at Brick & Mortar in Cambridge, Massachusetts.

TODD THRASHER is a managing partner at several bars in Alexandria, Virginia, including Restaurant Eve.

HIDETSUGU UENO owns Bar High Five in Tokyo.

FRANÇOIS VERA is the bar manager at Pour Vous in Los Angeles.

THAD VOGLER is the owner of Bar Agricole in San Francisco.

JAMES WAMPLER tends bar at Eleanor's in Smyrna, Georgia.

PHILIP WARD is the owner of Mayahuel in New York City.

THOMAS WAUGH oversees the cocktail program at ZZ's Clam Bar in New York City.

ANGUS WINCHESTER owns Alconomics, a cocktail consulting company.

DAMIAN WINDSOR is a bartender and cocktail consultant based in Los Angeles. He recently created the cocktail programs at Warwick and Tiki No.

HAL WOLIN, a partner at The Cocktail Guru consulting company, writes the spirits blog A Muddled Thought.

DAVID WONDRICH is a cocktail and spirits writer and historian. He is Esquire magazine's drinks correspondent and has written several books, including Imbibe! and Punch: The Delights (and Dangers) of the Flowing Bowl.

DUSHAN ZARIC is a co-owner of Employees Only and Macao Trading Company in New York City. He is also a cofounder of The 86 Co. spirits.

Thank you

In addition to everyone who contributed recipes, the following people were indispensable in making this book possible: Greg Best, Jamie Boudreau, Sean Frederick, Jeff Grdinich, Pip Hanson, Bobby Heugel, Sean Hoard, Valerie Meehan, Lindsay Nader, Travis Reese, Brooks Reitz and Mike Ryan.

More books from

FOOD & WINE

Annual Cookbook
An entire year of FOOD & WINE recipes.

Best of the Best Cookbook Recipes
The best recipes from the 25 best cookbooks of the year.

Wine Guide
Pocket-size guide with more than 1,000 recommendations.